soup's
on!

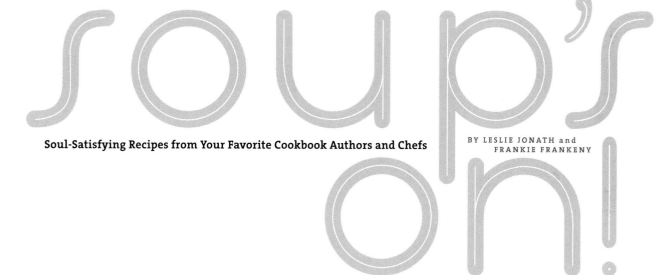

soup's on!

Soul-Satisfying Recipes from Your Favorite Cookbook Authors and Chefs

BY LESLIE JONATH and
FRANKIE FRANKENY

PHOTOGRAPHS BY FRANKIE FRANKENY

CHRONICLE BOOKS

SAN FRANCISCO

Library of Congress Cataloging-in-Publication Data available.

ISBN-10: 0-8118-5262-8
ISBN-13: 978-0-8118-5262-3

Manufactured in China

Designed by Julia Flagg
Food styling by Alison Richman, Matt Brimer, and Joey Altman

10 9 8 7 6 5 4 3 2

Chronicle Books LLC
680 Second Street
San Francisco, California 94107

www.chroniclebooks.com

"Soup is cuisine's kindest course.
It breathes reassurance; it steams consolation;
after a weary day it promotes sociability...
there is nothing like a bowl of hot soup,
its wisp of aromatic steam making the nostrils
quiver with anticipation."

LOUIS P. DE GOUY, *The Soup Book*, 1949

I founded Nextcourse in 2003 as a way for chefs to bring their skill and passion to making delicious and nutritional food available to everyone in the community. Today, Nextcourse works with women in the San Francisco County Jail, and with high school students in the Mission. Both programs start by teaching participants the importance of healthful food for the physical and mental well-being of adults and children, and then shows them how to purchase food and prepare tasty, nutritious meals with little money and limited time. Our Mission High School program partners with Pie Ranch to bring urban students insight into the value of a vital rural farm community. Most recently I founded the Food from the Parks program to collaborate with state and national park services to increase the amount of local, sustainably produced food available to park visitors.

Over the last thirty years, I have had the pleasure of working with some of the best chefs in America. Many of them have participated directly with Nextcourse in our jail and youth programs. Others have made their contributions through similarly important efforts. This book brings together many of these thoughtful people. They have graciously donated their time and talent to create recipes for this book that show that great food—food that nourishes both body and soul—can be prepared at home economically. And the key ingredient found in every one of these recipes is a large amount of love.

Our chefs use ingredients produced with love by farmers and fishers who care not only about what they harvest but also about the planet. As you prepare the soups and stews in the following pages, I hope that you will come to appreciate the important connection that exists between the people who harvest the food and all of us who eat it. I hope, too, that you will discover healthful, delicious recipes that you will want to make again and again.. **LARRY BAIN,** founder, Nextcourse

We love soups and stews. Nothing soothes the soul like a steaming bowl of chicken soup, dashes winter's chill like a spicy beef stew, or takes us back to childhood like a creamy tomato bisque.

Soup is the most versatile of dishes. It can be humble or elegant, long-simmering or nearly instant, rich or light, smooth or chunky, creamy or brothy, piping hot or chilled. It can be served as an appetizer or a meal in a bowl, as an intimate dinner for two, or a feast for a dozen. It can be made year-round with all kinds of ingredients—from canned beans to farmers' market greens. It crosses cultures and economic lines, turning up on both modest dinner tables and in fancy dining rooms around the world.

And nothing draws a community around the table like a soup or stew. In a folktale that describes the origins of the now-legendary stone soup, three tired and hungry soldiers—or two weary travelers on a pilgrimage, depending on who is relating the tale—stop for the night in a poor village where the residents have little food. The visitors set an iron pot over a small wood fire in the central square, fill the pot with water, place a large stone in the bottom, and then announce that they are making stone soup. One villager points out that a soup flavored with just a stone will taste bland, and offers to bring a little cabbage for the pot. Soon other villagers begin contributing meager ingredients, and in time there is enough soup to feed everyone in the village. The soup turns out to be delicious and filling, but more importantly, it brings everyone together.

In the same way that the complex flavor of the stone soup was created by the individual contributions of the villagers, the rich content of this book draws on the collective generosity of dozens of people. In the following pages, you will find everything from classic cream soups to chunky chowders to rustic stews, all of them from the kitchens of chefs and cookbook authors who share a true community spirit.

In that same spirit of community, we are donating a portion of the proceeds from the sale of this book to Nextcourse, a San Francisco–based nonprofit food and nutrition educational organization. Started by chefs and restaurateurs in an effort to combat the acute food crisis in low-income neighborhoods, Nextcourse offers instruction in sound nutrition to individuals and community child-care providers. It also works with young people to create future leaders who will help challenge the food policies that limit accessibility to quality food in their communities.

We hope this book will inspire you to collect your own favorite recipes and build your own community of soup lovers. A soup kitchen creates food for those in need, but soup itself can create a community.

broths and stocks

1

Great soup begins with great stock. If the stock is flavorful and balanced, then the soup will also be flavorful and balanced. Because making stock is an inexact science, there are as many stock and broth recipes as there are cooks and cooking styles. The basic idea is to extract flavor from the best ingredients by simmering them in liquid over a long period of time.

What is the difference between a stock and a broth? The CIA (Culinary Institute of America) distinguishes broth and stock this way: Broths are intended to be served as (or clarified to make) consommé, whereas stocks are used to make other dishes (sauces, soups, stews, braises, etc.). Meat and poultry broths have more pronounced flavor than their stock counterparts. By the same token, broths lack the gelatin from the bones. Stocks are typically simmered longer than broths, too. Having noted this, it should be said that many recipes use these terms interchangeably. Most of the recipes in this book call for stock unless otherwise noted; broths generally refer to commercially available products. In some cases the soups in this book provide a broth or stock as part of the overall recipe.

You might have your own favorite stocks, but we've provided simple recipes for chicken, beef, fish, and vegetarian stocks, as well as a recipe on how to doctor store-bought stocks and broths. Since true soup fiends will always have a container of stock in the refrigerator, the following stock recipes are for more than you would need for a single soup. To store the extra stock, once it's cooked and cooled, strain into a container (preferably with a storage capacity of 1 to 2 quarts) and refrigerate overnight. The fat will rise to the top and you can lift it off. Cover and refrigerate for up to three days. Stock will keep in the freezer for up to three months.

Of course, it's not always possible to make stock from scratch, so, in a pinch, store-bought is a convenient replacement. Most canned store-bought products are labeled "broth" and will have sodium, so when using them, you should taste your soup before adding additional salt. Some specialty shops keep high-quality stocks or stock bases in the freezer section. We recommend you seek these out whenever possible.

chicken stock

MAKES **6** QUARTS

- **3 pounds chicken necks and backs**
- **1 pound chicken wings**
- **2 white** or **yellow onions,** sliced
- **2 carrots,** scrubbed, cut into ½-inch slices
- **2 stalks celery,** cut into thirds
- **4 sprigs fresh thyme**
- **4 sprigs fresh flat-leaf parsley**
- **2 dried** or **fresh bay leaves**
- **1 teaspoon whole black peppercorns**

Place all the ingredients in a large stockpot. Add 4 to 4½ quarts of cold water to the stockpot, or to cover. Bring to a boil over high heat. Reduce heat to low and simmer for 45 minutes. Skim off the skin that forms on the surface with a spoon and discard. Simmer the stock for 3 hours on the lowest heat possible, skimming as needed.

Strain the stock through a sieve or a colander into a large bowl. Discard the solids and let the liquid cool to room temperature. Transfer to airtight containers. The stock may be refrigerated for up to 3 days or frozen for up to 3 months.

beef stock

MAKES **4** QUARTS

- **5 pounds beef bones,** sawed into smaller pieces
- **1 pound beef stew meat,** cubed
- **2 cups dry red wine**
- **1 can** (12 ounces) **whole tomatoes**
- **1 large onion, with peel,** quartered
- **2 large carrots,** cut into thirds
- **2 stalks celery,** cut into thirds
- **8 sprigs fresh flat-leaf parsley**
- **6 sprigs fresh thyme** or ¾ **teaspoon dried thyme**
- **4 sprigs fresh rosemary** or
  2 teaspoons dried rosemary
- **2 dried** or **fresh bay leaves**
- **1 tablespoon whole black peppercorns**

Place all the ingredients in a large stockpot. Add 6 quarts of cold water to the stockpot, or to cover. Bring to a boil over high heat. Reduce heat to low and simmer. Skim the foam from the surface and discard. Simmer over the lowest possible heat for about 3½ hours. Skim off the skin that forms on the surface with a spoon and discard. Add water if the level drops below the bones.

Strain the stock through a sieve or colander into a large bowl or into another large pot. Discard the solids and let the liquid cool to room temperature. Transfer the stock to airtight containers. The stock may be refrigerated for up to 3 days or frozen for up to 3 months.

NOTE: To make a dark roasted-flavored stock, roast all the components on a baking sheet at 400 degrees F until well browned, about 45 minutes. Proceed with the recipe as directed.

fish stock

MAKES **4** QUARTS

4 pounds heads and bones of non-oily white fish such as sole, flounder, snapper, or bass

3 tablespoons olive oil

1 onion, cut into ¼-inch slices

2 medium carrots cut into ¼-inch slices

2 stalks celery, cut into ¼-inch slices

½ fennel bulb, cut into ¼-inch slices, or **1 teaspoon fennel seeds**

2 fresh or **dried bay leaves**

4 whole garlic cloves

8 sprigs fresh flat-leaf parsley

10 sprigs fresh thyme

8 whole black peppercorns

1 cup dry white wine

Remove the gills and any traces of blood from the fish heads. Thoroughly wash the bones and cut them to fit into a 12-quart stockpot. Put the heads and bones in a bowl and set aside.

Heat the oil in a large pot over medium-high heat. Then add the onion, carrots, celery, fennel, bay leaves, garlic, parsley, thyme, and peppercorns. Cover and cook until the vegetables are tender, 8 to 10 minutes.

Increase the heat to high and add the fish heads and bones. Cook, stirring, for 10 minutes. Add the wine and reduce by half. Add approximately 6 quarts of cold water to the stockpot, or to cover. Bring to a boil. Reduce the heat to low and simmer until the stock is flavorful, about 30 minutes, skimming any film that rises to the surface. Turn off the heat and let sit for 10 minutes.

Strain the stock through a fine sieve or colander set over a large bowl. Discard the solids and let the liquid cool to room temperature. Transfer to airtight containers. Refrigerate and use the stock within 1 day or freeze for up to 3 months.

vegetable stock

MAKES **4** QUARTS

1 tablespoon olive oil

1 large onion, coarsely chopped

2 carrots, coarsely chopped

2 large parsnips, coarsely chopped

2 zucchini or **yellow squash**

1 stalk celery, coarsely chopped

1 large tomato

1 garlic bulb (with skin), cut in half

Several sprigs fresh thyme

Several sprigs fresh flat-leaf parsley

1 dried bay leaf

Heat the oil in a medium stockpot over medium-high heat. Add the onion and cook, stirring until translucent, 8 to 10 minutes. Add the carrots, parsnips, zucchini, celery, tomato, and garlic. Cook until tender, about 15 minutes.

Add 4 quarts of cold water, the thyme, parsley, and bay leaf. Bring to a boil, reduce the heat, and simmer until the broth is well flavored, about 1 hour.

Strain the stock through a sieve or colander, pressing the vegetables to extract any juices. Discard the vegetables and let the liquid cool to room temperature. Transfer to airtight containers. The stock can be refrigerated for up to 3 days or frozen for up to 3 months.

store-bought broth made better

MAKES **4½** CUPS

1 can (10 ounces) **chicken broth, beef broth,** or **clam juice**

2 stalks celery with leaves, thinly sliced

2 carrots, thinly sliced

1 onion, thinly sliced

½ fennel bulb, thinly sliced

10 sprigs fresh flat-leaf parsley

1 dried bay leaf

2 to 3 sprigs fresh thyme

Put all the ingredients in a medium stockpot. Add 1 quart of cold water to the stockpot, or to cover. Bring to a boil, then reduce the heat and simmer until the flavors have melded, about 25 minutes.

Strain the stock through a sieve or colander set over a large bowl. Discard the solids and let the liquid cool to room temperature. Transfer to airtight containers. The stock may be refrigerated for up to 3 days or frozen for up to 3 months.

vegetable and vegetarian soups 2

artichoke soup
with tapenade

SERVES
6

Loretta Keller makes this savory soup for her Greek friend Zoi and for Jennifer Biesty, her chef at COCO500 in San Francisco when artichokes are at their peak in California in March and April. She serves it as a starter to a Greek spring-festival feast that includes grilled lamb, asparagus, eggplant, lots of crisp wine, and laughter. You can make the tapenade using a variety of prepared olive pastes such as niçoise, calamata, or picholine. The tapenade is also delicious slathered on crusty Italian bread.

TAPENADE

3 anchovy fillets, rinsed and chopped

2 ounces prepared olive paste

½ orange, zested and juiced

¼ lemon, zested

2 teaspoons chopped fresh oregano or **marjoram**

1 teaspoon chopped brined or rinsed, salt-packed capers

1 small garlic clove, finely chopped

SOUP

½ cup extra-virgin olive oil, plus more for drizzling

2 yellow onions, diced

½ cup sliced garlic

Salt

1 cup dry white wine

2 quarts Chicken Stock (page 13) or **water**

1 cup short-grain rice

15 medium to large artichoke hearts, thickly sliced or cubed

4 egg yolks

½ cup freshly squeezed lemon juice (preferably Meyer lemon)

Freshly ground black pepper

TO MAKE THE TAPENADE, mix all the ingredients together until well blended. Set aside until ready to serve.

TO MAKE THE SOUP, in a sauté pan over medium heat, warm the ½ cup oil and cook the onions and garlic until tender; season with salt to taste. Add the wine and continue to cook until the wine is reduced by half, about 5 minutes. Add the stock and rice and cook until the rice is tender. Add the artichokes. Cook until the artichokes are tender, approximately 15 minutes. In a separate bowl, whisk together the egg yolks and lemon juice. To finish the soup, whisk this mixture into the soup. Adjust the seasoning with salt, pepper, and more olive oil if desired. Divide the soup among 6 bowls. Garnish each bowl with a dollop of tapenade.

maytag cheddar soup

The folks at Maytag Farms, while famous for their blue cheese, have also made a white Cheddar cheese on and off through the years. That cheese became the inspiration for a soup recipe adapted by Laura Werlin for her book *The New American Cheese.* Unlike many ultrathick Cheddar cheese soups, this one is light in texture—but don't be fooled, since it couldn't be richer. To make the best, most flavorful soup, use unsalted stock or broth and an aged, but not super-sharp, Cheddar.

4 tablespoons (2 ounces) **unsalted butter**

6 scallions, chopped

3 stalks celery, diced

2 carrots, diced

¼ cup all-purpose flour

5 cups unsalted Chicken Stock (page 13) or **broth**

1 large russet potato, peeled and diced

1 cup milk or **half-and-half**

8 ounces Cheddar cheese, preferably white, coarsely grated

1 teaspoon Tabasco sauce

1 teaspoon Worcestershire sauce

Salt

In a large pot, melt the butter over medium-low heat. Add the scallions, celery, and carrots and cook until limp, about 10 minutes. Sprinkle the flour over the vegetables, stir, and cook for 3 minutes. Add the stock, 1 cup at a time, stirring constantly. Add the potato. Bring to a boil and then reduce the heat to a simmer. Cook until the potato is soft, 20 to 30 minutes. At this point, you can purée the soup base in a blender or you can leave it chunky. A purée will result in a thicker soup, while the non-puréed version provides a variety of textures. Both taste good.

Whisk in the milk, cheese, Tabasco, and Worcestershire. Taste and add salt, if needed. Serve immediately.

asparagus and rice soup
with pancetta and black pepper

SERVES **4** FOR AN APPETIZER; **2** FOR AN ENTRÉE

This simple soup from *The Zuni Cafe Cookbook* by Judy Rodgers, chef/owner of San Francisco's Zuni Cafe, is crowded with flavors and textures. The ingredients are dosed to strike a high-pitched balance between the sweet onion and asparagus and the pungent pancetta and pepper. The mild, tender rice mediates. You can use jumbo, medium, or skinny asparagus spears, as long as they are perky and sweet. Choose spears with neat, tight tips and bright, firm stalks. Judy uses Carnaroli or arborio rice for this soup, because she usually has it in-house for risotto, but you can use any type of white rice you like, and gauge the cooking time accordingly. This soup pairs nicely with Penfold's Eden Valley Reserve Riesling, 2000.

6 tablespoons extra-virgin olive oil, divided

2 cups diced yellow onions

Salt

¼ cup white rice

About 3½ cups Chicken Stock (page 13) or **broth**

About 8 ounces asparagus, woody ends trimmed

3 to 4 ounces pancetta, finely minced (½ to ⅔ cup)

Freshly cracked black pepper

Warm about 4 tablespoons of the oil in a 4-quart saucepan over medium-low heat. Add the onions and a pinch of salt and cook slowly, stirring regularly. Don't let the onions color; they should "sweat" their moisture and then become tender and translucent in about 10 minutes. Add the rice, stock, and ½ cup water and bring to a simmer. Cover tightly and cook until the rice is nutty-tender, 15 to 20 minutes, depending on the rice you choose. The broth will be cloudy and should taste sweet from the onions. Turn off the heat.

While the rice is cooking, sliver the asparagus, slicing it at an angle about ⅛ inch thick. Don't worry if the slivers vary a little in thickness; the irregularity will guarantee uneven cooking and a pleasantly varied texture. You should get about 2 cups.

Warm the remaining 2 tablespoons of oil in a 12-inch skillet over medium heat. Add the pancetta and asparagus slivers and stir once to coat, then spread out and leave to sizzle until those at the edges of the pan begin to color. Toss or stir once, then leave to color again. Repeat a few times until the mass has softened and shrunk by about one-third.

Scrape the pancetta and asparagus into the broth and bring to a boil. Add lots of pepper. Boil for about 1 minute. This soup is best when served promptly, while all the flavors are still bold and the texture varied.

curried squash and apple soup

SERVES **4** TO **6** AS A MAIN COURSE, OR **8** AS A FIRST COURSE

This vegetarian soup, from Barbara Kafka's book *Soup: A Way of Life,* can be a silky and succulent first course for a fall or winter evening, but she prefers to serve it as a main course with boiled rice on the side and a sprinkling of raisins and slivered almonds on top, alongside a lovely chutney

2 medium acorn squash, cut in half lengthwise, and seeds and fibers removed

¼ cup vegetable oil

4 teaspoons black mustard seeds

3 tablespoons curry powder

2 large Granny Smith or other tart apples, quartered, cored, cut into 1-inch cubes, and tossed with the juice of 1 lime

1 medium onion, cut into chunks

10 medium garlic cloves, smashed and peeled

1½ tablespoons very finely chipped peeled ginger

4 cups Vegetable Broth (recipe follows)

Lime juice, to taste

2 teaspoons kosher salt

FOR SERVING

1 lime, sliced across into very thin rounds

¾ cup yogurt

Heat the oven to 500 degrees F. Roast the squash cut-side up in a roasting pan for 50 minutes, or until soft. Scoop the pulp from the squash.

In a medium saucepan, stir together the vegetable oil and mustard seeds over medium heat until the seeds are popping (be careful—it is very easy to burn the spices if the oil gets too hot). Stir in the curry powder and cook, stirring constantly, over medium-low heat for about 1½ minutes.

Stir in the apples, squash, onion, garlic, ginger, and broth. Bring to a boil. Lower the heat. Simmer for 20 minutes, or until the apples and onion are soft.

In a food processor, working in batches, purée the soup; or pass through the medium disc of a food mill. The soup can be made ahead to this point and refrigerated for up to 3 days.

Return the soup to the pot and heat through. Season with the lime juice and salt. Top each serving with a thin slice of lime and a dollop of yogurt.

vegetable broth

MAKES **8** CUPS

For a smoother, more unctuous mouth feel, agar-agar or tapioca powder may be added to the finished broth.

2 garlic cloves, smashed and peeled

2 medium to large onions, quartered

3 medium carrots, peeled and cut into 1-inch lengths

3 medium tomatoes, coarsely chopped

3 medium leeks, white part only, cut in half lengthwise, washed well, and cut across into 1-inch lengths

2 tablespoons olive oil

1 medium bunch spinach, stemmed, washed well, and cut across into 2-inch strips

1 cup celery leaves

Stems from 2 bunches parsley (reserve the leaves for another use)

2 bay leaves

8 cups water

To make a roasted vegetable broth, place a rack in the middle of oven and heat the oven to 500 degree F.

In a large roasting pan, place the garlic, onions, carrots, tomatoes, and leeks. Add the olive oil and toss to coat. Roast for 15 minutes. Turn the vegetables and roast for 15 more minutes. Move the vegetables around in the pan and roast for 10 more minutes, or until all the vegetables are nicely browned and the tomatoes are collapsing.

Place the roasted vegetables in a tall narrow stockpot. Add the spinach, celery leaves, parsley stems, and bay leaves, and 7 cups of the water. Place the roasting pan on top of the stove. Stir in the remaining water. Bring to a boil, scraping up any browned bits from the sides and bottom of the pan with a wooden spoon. Pour this liquid over the vegetables in the pot.

For a plain vegetable broth, place all the ingredients, including the water, in a tall narrow stockpot. Bring to a boil. Lower the heat and simmer, partially covered, for 45 minutes. Strain through a damp cloth–lined sieve. Use immediately, refrigerate for up to 3 days, or freeze for up to 3 months.

NOTE: To add consistency, ½ cup agar-agar flakes (8 teaspoons powdered) or 5 tablespoons tapioca powder may be added to the finished broth. Mix together the agar-agar, if using, and the broth and bring to a boil. Lower the heat and simmer until the agar-agar dissolves, about 5 minutes. If using tapioca, mix with ¼ cup cold broth. Bring the rest of the broth to a boil. Whisk in the tapioca. Return to a boil. Remove from the stove. Both of these are good. The agar-agar sets up at room temperature.

carrot soup

Carrots are closely related to parsley and fennel, and they contribute a sweet, rich character to most of the stocks, marinades, soups, and sauces made at the legendary Chez Panisse in Berkeley, California. But their particular charms are most apparent when they are cooked alone or with a few other vegetables. This soup by Alice Waters is best made in the middle to late summer, when there is great abundance of fresh, sweet carrots.

4 tablespoons (2 ounces) **unsalted butter**

2 onions, sliced

1 sprig fresh thyme

2½ pounds carrots, peeled and thinly sliced

2 teaspoons salt

6 cups Chicken Stock (page 13) or **light chicken broth** (made using ½ regular stock and ½ water)

Melt the butter in a heavy-bottomed pot. Add the onions and thyme. Cook over medium-low heat until tender, about 10 minutes. Add the carrots and season with the salt. Cook for 5 minutes (cooking the carrots with the onions for a while concentrates the flavor). Add the stock, bring to a boil, lower the heat, and simmer until the carrots are tender, about 30 minutes. When done, season with salt to taste and ladle into bowls to serve.

VARIATIONS:

* For a lighter, simpler version, skip the preliminary sautéing of the onions and instead, add them directly to the broth with the carrots, and simmer until tender.

* For a more delicate soup dominated by the pure flavor of carrots, make the soup with water or half water and half broth, and purée with a food mill or blender before serving.

* Garnish with a bit of whipped cream or crème fraîche seasoned with salt, pepper, and chopped herbs. Chervil, chives, or tarragon are all good choices.

* Add ¼ cup basmati rice with the carrots, use water instead of stock, add 1 cup of plain yogurt just before puréeing, and garnish with mint.

* Cook a jalapeño pepper with the onions; add some cilantro before puréeing, and garnish with chopped cilantro.

* Heat some clarified butter or olive oil, sizzle a spoonful of cumin seeds in it, and spoon this over the soup as a garnish.

gingery cauliflower soup
Gobi Ka

SERVES **4** TO **6**

This soup by Madhur Jaffrey, from her book *Quick & Easy Indian Cooking,* may be served as an elegant first course or as part of a simple lunch. It may be made a day in advance and refrigerated. Reheat gently. It is a good idea to have the cumin, coriander, turmeric, and cayenne pepper all measured into a small bowl before you start, as they go in together and cook very briefly.

3 tablespoons vegetable oil

1 medium onion, chopped

1-inch piece fresh ginger, peeled and cut into fine slivers

4 garlic cloves, chopped

2 teaspoons ground coriander

1 teaspoon ground cumin

¼ teaspoon ground turmeric

⅛ to ¼ teaspoon cayenne pepper

5 cups Chicken Stock (page 13) or broth

2 medium potatoes, peeled and cut into rough ⅓-inch dice

2 heaping cups (8 ounces) cauliflower florets

Salt

⅔ cup heavy whipping cream

Heat the oil over medium-high heat in a large saucepan. When hot, put in the onion, ginger, and garlic. Stir and fry until the onion is somewhat browned, about 4 minutes. Put in the coriander, cumin, turmeric, and cayenne. Stir once and put in the stock, potatoes, and cauliflower. If the stock is unsalted, put in ¾ teaspoon salt. Stir and bring to a boil. Cover, turn the heat to low, and simmer gently until the potatoes are tender, about 10 minutes. Taste for salt, adding more if you like.

Put the soup into a blender, in 2 batches or more as required, and blend thoroughly. Strain, pushing down to get all the pulp; discard the solids. Add the cream and mix. The soup may now be reheated over low heat and served.

garlicky cucumber-yogurt soup
for a sweltering day in the Mediterranean

SERVES 4 TO 6

Marlena Spieler, columnist for the *San Francisco Chronicle* and author of *Grilled Cheese*, likens this cold cucumber soup to Greek *tzadziki* dip. It's even better the next day and can be thinned with water for a cooling drinklike appetizer soup. This recipe is quite garlicky, but you can adjust the amount of garlic according to your taste. Greek yogurt is thicker, richer, and more full of milky flavor. Unlike a regular cucumber, a European cucumber is seedless and the skin is tender and not bitter so you don't have to peel it.

1 seedless European cucumber (12 to 14 ounces), unpeeled, diced

2 to 3 tablespoons chopped fresh dill, plus extra for garnish

2 to 3 tablespoons chopped fresh mint

1 to 2 garlic cloves or more, depending on your taste

Salt

1 cup full-fat plain Greek yogurt or **sour cream,** plus extra for garnish

1 cup low-fat plain yogurt

1 lemon, juiced

2 tablespoons extra-virgin olive oil

3 tablespoons coarsely chopped walnuts

In a food processor, add approximately ⅔ of the diced cucumber with the dill, mint, garlic, and 1 to 2 teaspoons of salt and pulse until roughly combined. Add 1 cup cold water and pulse to blend to an even purée, 20 to 30 seconds.

Add the Greek yogurt and low-fat yogurt and blend until smooth, then add the lemon juice and olive oil and blend again.

Season with salt to taste (be generous; the soup will be cold and takes a little more salt than you'd think) and chill until cold. Serve garnished with a dollop of Greek yogurt, a sprinkling of the reserved diced cucumber, fresh dill, and coarsely chopped walnuts.

classic andalusian gazpacho

SERVES **4** TO **6**

Andalusian gazpacho is a simple, delicious combination of the region's key ingredients—primarily bread, tomatoes, bell peppers, and garlic. It's nutritious and delightfully refreshing. This version, by food writer and Barcelona resident Jeff Koehler, is a classic one that he makes at home for his family. Sometimes, when summer heats up, he leaves out the bread, thins the soup with cold water, pours it into a jug, and keeps it in the refrigerator to drink by the glass. The key to great gazpacho is using the ripest, freshest tomatoes available. Peel and seed them over a bowl to capture all of the flavorful juices.

One 1-inch slice day-old crustless country bread

1 small garlic clove, peeled

Salt

2½ pounds ripe tomatoes, peeled, seeded, and quartered, all juices reserved

1 green bell pepper, seeded and cut into pieces

1 medium cucumber, peeled and cut into pieces

¼ cup extra-virgin olive oil

1 tablespoon sherry vinegar

Freshly ground black pepper

GARNISHES

Chopped hard-boiled eggs

Finely chopped red bell pepper

Finely chopped green bell pepper

Finely chopped onion, preferably sweet

Finely chopped cucumber

Plain croutons

Tear the bread into pieces and submerge it in 1 cup of cold water. Press the bread down so that it absorbs the liquid.

Pound the garlic with 2 generous pinches of salt in a mortar, and then transfer it to a blender. In 2 batches if necessary, add the tomatoes, bell pepper, and cucumber to the blender, and blend until smooth. Gently squeeze the water from the bread, reserving the water. Add the bread to the blender as well as the oil and blend until the gazpacho is creamy smooth, with a uniform color. Thin with water, beginning with the reserved water from the bread, until the desired consistency is found.

Pour the gazpacho into a serving bowl and refrigerate it until the mixture is thoroughly chilled, at least 90 minutes. Prepare the garnishes.

Before serving, stir the vinegar into the gazpacho and season with salt and pepper to taste. Stir well and pour into individual bowls. Serve with the garnishes on a plate in the middle, allowing everyone to sprinkle them as desired on top of their gazpacho.

silky roasted yellow pepper soup

SERVES **4** TO **6** AS A FIRST COURSE

When visiting the North Farmers' Market in Columbus, Ohio, one late September, Deborah Madison, author of *The Greens Cookbook* and *Vegetable Soups from Deborah Madison's Kitchen,* happily filled a bag with huge golden peppers to take home with her. This soup, from her book *Local Flavors,* is a little laborious to make, but you don't need to serve a lot of it—just a taste at the start of the meal. And there are many ways you can finish this soup—with a vinegar reduction, romesco sauce spread on small croutons, sour cream and chives, a salsa verde, or with the garnish of tiny minced peppers. And you can serve it hot or chilled.

You can quickly throw together a pepper soup using the same ingredients if you don't bother to peel or roast the peppers. Just sauté them with the onions, add water or stock, and you're done. However, it's the skins that give peppers a sharp, unpleasant taste, so Deborah takes extra time with this soup, halving and broiling the peppers first until the skins bubble (but don't char) or simply peeling them. While the broiler is heating, she uses the pepper cores and a few fall vegetables to make a simple, flavor-enhancing stock.

STOCK

2 teaspoons olive oil

1 small onion, sliced

The cores and trimmings from the bell peppers (see below)

1 small zucchini, chopped

1 small carrot, chopped

A handful of small, ripe tomatoes or **1 large tomato,** halved

A few fresh basil sprigs or **leaves**

1 pinch fresh thyme

Sea salt

SOUP

2 pounds (4 to 5) meaty yellow bell peppers, tops sliced off, cores and seeds removed and reserved, plus **2 tablespoons finely diced raw bell peppers,** different colors

Olive oil, as needed

1 small red onion, thinly sliced (about 1 cup)

Vinegar, such as Chardonnay, sherry, or balsamic

Preheat the broiler and position a rack about 8 inches beneath the broiling unit.

TO MAKE THE STOCK, heat the oil in a pot over medium heat, add the onion and the pepper cores, zucchini, carrot, and tomatoes as you slice them, along with the basil, thyme, and a scant teaspoon of salt. When the onion has some color, add 5 cups water, bring to a boil, then simmer partially covered until you're ready for the stock, or about 25 minutes. Strain; discard the solids.

TO MAKE THE SOUP, cut the 2 pounds of bell peppers in half, lengthwise, and flatten them. Brush the skins with oil, including the tops (minus their stems), and place them skin-side up on a baking sheet. Broil only until the skin is bubbling, puckered, and light brown. Put them in a bowl, cover, and leave them to steam for at least 15 minutes.

Meanwhile, heat 1½ tablespoons of oil in a soup pot. Add the onion and cook over low heat while you peel the peppers. Pull or scrape off as much skin as you can without making yourself crazy, then chop and add the peppers to the pot as you go, along with ½ teaspoon salt and the strained stock. Bring to a boil and simmer, covered, for 20 minutes. Cool slightly, then purée in batches; for the best texture, pass the soup through a food mill. Taste for salt and add a few drops of vinegar to bring everything together. Serve with a spoonful of the diced pepper scattered over each bowl.

fresh pea, leek, and mint soup

You'll find all the tastes of spring in this delicate, aromatic soup by Los Angeles writer Jessica Strand, author of the entertaining books *Dinner Parties* and *Intimate Gatherings*. The soup is a lovely way to feature fresh peas, but feel free to use frozen petite green peas if you're not in the mood for shelling.

4 tablespoons olive oil

1 tablespoon unsalted butter

4 medium leeks, white parts only, coarsely chopped

2 small heads Boston lettuce, cored and separated

½ cup coarsely chopped fresh mint, plus **8 fresh mint leaves**

5½ cups Chicken Stock (page 13) or **broth**

3 cups fresh or **frozen green peas**

1 Meyer lemon, juiced

Sea salt

Freshly ground black pepper

¾ cup crème fraîche

Heat the oil and butter in a stockpot over medium-low heat. Add the leeks and cook until they are soft, 7 to 10 minutes.

Add the lettuce and chopped mint to the pot and cook, stirring constantly, for 2 to 3 minutes, until the leaves are wilted. Add the stock and peas. Bring to a boil, then reduce the heat to low and simmer, uncovered, until the flavors have melded, 10 to 12 minutes.

Remove the soup from the stove. Use a hand-held mixer or blender to purée the soup until smooth. If using a standard blender, add the soup in batches. When the soup is completely puréed, reheat it over low heat. Add the lemon juice, salt, and pepper to taste and stir to blend.

Ladle the soup into 4 bowls, add a dollop of crème fraîche, and garnish each serving with 2 mint leaves.

onion soup gratinée

In this country-style onion soup by Jacques Pépin from his book *Simple and Healthy Cooking*, Jacques cooks the onions until they turn a rich, dark color and take on an intense flavor. Then he purées a little of the finished soup and stirs it into the remainder to thicken it slightly. If you prefer, all of the finished soup can be pulsed in a food processor to give it the texture of a light onion purée. Or you can serve the soup plain (not puréed and without the cheese and final browning in the oven), just with a garnish of croutons.

In the gratinée version, the finished soup should have a beautiful golden crust of bread and cheese, achieved here with only a quarter of the cheese used in conventional recipes for this classic soup. This is a satisfying dish, and the mixture of lean mozzarella and good Swiss (Gruyère) cheese makes a nice combination.

1 tablespoon extra-virgin olive oil

6 to 8 medium onions (about 2 pounds), thinly sliced (about 8 cups)

5 cups Chicken Stock (page 13) or lower-salt chicken broth

Freshly ground black pepper

16 to 18 thin slices French-style baguette

½ cup shredded part-skim mozzarella cheese

¼ cup shredded Gruyère cheese

Heat the oil in a large, heavy pot. When it is hot, add the onions. Cover and cook over high heat for 5 minutes. Uncover and cook over medium heat until the onions are well browned, about 15 minutes. Add the stock, 2 cups water, and pepper to taste. Cover and cook for 20 minutes.

Meanwhile, preheat the oven to 400 degrees F. Arrange the bread slices in a single layer on a baking sheet. Bake the bread slices until they are brown, about 10 minutes. Set aside for use as croutons while you finish the soup.

Transfer about one-third of the cooked soup to the bowl of a food processor and purée it. Add the purée to the remaining soup in the pot.

To serve the soup, pour it into a large ovenproof crock (or divide it among 6 individual crocks). Top with croutons, then sprinkle on the mozzarella and Gruyère. Place the crock(s) on a baking sheet and bake until the cheese is melted and the top is browned, about 35 minutes. If needed, place under the broiler for 5 minutes to brown the cheeses and create a crusty top on the soup. Serve immediately.

mâche and parmesan soup

SERVES
4

This simple recipe by Georgeanne Brennan, adapted from her book *Great Greens*, features *mâche*, a delicious delicate green. The mâche wilts into the soup, retaining its petal shape and slightly peppery taste, while the Parmesan provides complexity for the broth. Serving the soup spooned over garlic-rubbed, Parmesan-topped toasts adds body and reinforces the flavors. Watercress or spinach may be used instead of mâche, or even baby arugula.

4 medium-thick slices baguette or
other sturdy country bread

1½ tablespoons extra-virgin olive oil

1 garlic clove, peeled

4 cups Chicken Stock (page 13) or **broth**

2 tablespoons dry white wine

1 ounce chunk Parmesan cheese with rind

1 cup mâche or **delicate spring greens**

¼ cup freshly grated Parmesan cheese

Preheat the broiler. Place the slices of baguette on a broiler pan and broil until golden, 5 to 7 minutes. Remove from the broiler and drizzle with the oil. Rub the garlic across the surface of the toasts. The irregular, crisp surface of the toast acts like a grater. Set aside.

Put the stock in a large saucepan and add the wine. Bring to a boil, and boil uncovered to reduce by a tablespoon or two, 3 to 5 minutes. Add the Parmesan rind and reduce the heat to low. Simmer, covered, until the cheese has begun to melt a bit and the broth is flavored by it, about 25 minutes. Add the mâche and cook another 2 minutes. Place a piece of toast in the bottom of each of 4 soup bowls. Sprinkle each toast with a tablespoon of the cheese, and then ladle the hot soup over the toast.

fall mushroom soup

SERVES
4

Nothing embodies the earthy flavors of autumn more than mushrooms. This soothing recipe, from *Comfort Me With Apples* by *Gourmet* editor in chief Ruth Reichl, is as delicious as it is simple to make. You can use simple button mushrooms or a combination of wild mushrooms such as chanterelles and porcini.

4 tablespoons (2 ounces) **unsalted butter**

1 small onion, diced

8 ounces fresh mushrooms, thinly sliced

¼ cup all-purpose flour

1 cup Beef Stock (page 13) or **broth**

2 cups half-and-half

¼ teaspoon ground nutmeg

1 bay leaf

Salt

Freshly ground black pepper

Melt the butter in a heavy sauté pan over medium-high heat. When the foam subsides, add the onion and sauté until golden. Add the mushrooms and sauté until brown. Stir in the flour, and then slowly add the stock, stirring constantly.

Heat the half-and-half in a saucepan over low heat or in the microwave. Add it to the mushrooms along with the nutmeg, bay leaf, and salt and pepper to taste. Cover and simmer over low heat until the flavors meld, about 10 minutes; do not boil. Remove the bay leaf and serve.

chilled beet borscht

Use red beets for this borscht by Gabrielle Hamilton, chef/owner of Prune restaurant in New York City. The outlandish crimson color is part of its appeal. While many people remark on the horseradish in the soup, it is actually the combination of Dijon mustard and yellow onion that gives the soup its peppery flavor. Gabrielle likes to make this soup in the summer when the beets are fresh and when she's overdosed on the ubiquitous gazpacho that saturates the "chilled soup" category on menus. Sour cream is an appropriate garnish, or drizzle a little heavy cream over each bowl.

8 pounds red beets

3 long European seedless cucumbers or **1³/₄ pounds green cucumbers,** peeled, cut in half lengthwise, and seeded with a teaspoon

3 yellow onions, cut into rough 1½-inch dice

4 cups sour cream, plus more for garnish

2 cups Dijon mustard

1¹/₃ cups balsamic vinegar

6 tablespoons sugar

Fresh sprigs dill, for garnish

Wash the beets well using a vegetable brush to remove any caked-on mud, dirt, and sand. Remove the stems and greens and reserve for another use. Place the beets in a large pot, cover with cold water, and bring to a boil. Reduce the heat so they are still boiling, but not raucously. Cook until tender (a skewer inserted in the center of each beet yields little resistance, keeping in mind that different-size beets cook at different times and also that once removed from the water the beets will continue to "cook" with their residual heat; overcooking diminishes flavor and color).

Drain the beets in a colander. When they are cool enough to handle, peel them completely. The skins should slip off easily. (If you are concerned about staining your fingers, wear a pair of latex gloves.)

Cut the beets into large, rough dice. (If you are concerned about staining your cutting board, cut the beets carefully in your gloved hand.)

In a large, nonreactive bowl (glass, stainless steel, or ceramic), combine the beets, cucumbers, onions, sour cream, mustard, vinegar, and sugar and mix well. This will look like a wet, purplish, chunky mystery salad at a bad potluck supper. Cover with plastic wrap and refrigerate a full 24 hours.

Place the mixture in the bowl of a food processor with the metal blade attachment and pulse until the soup is the consistency of coarse, wet sand. Serve well chilled, garnished with an additional spoonful of sour cream and a sprig of dill.

pappa col pomodoro
tomato-bread soup

SERVES **6** TO **8**

Chef Tony Mantuano created this simple recipe for Café Spiaggia, the more informal Italian restaurant in the Chicago-based Spiaggia restaurant family. Originally conceived as a way to utilize day-old bread, this classic Italian soup is an example of transforming a few simple ingredients into a superb dish.

3 tablespoons extra-virgin olive oil, plus extra for drizzling

1 small sweet onion, thinly sliced

2 garlic cloves, thinly sliced

3 pounds fresh Roma tomatoes, peeled and seeded, or **two 28-ounce cans plum tomatoes with 1½ cans of the juice**

1 loaf crusty, country-style bread (about 1 pound)

Sea salt

Freshly ground black pepper

1 cup grated high-quality Parmesan cheese, such as Parmigiano-Reggiano, plus more for passing at the table

Fresh basil leaves, for garnish

In a medium stockpot over medium-low heat, heat the oil and cook the onion and garlic until translucent, 15 to 20 minutes. Add the tomatoes, increase the heat to medium, and lightly simmer for 1 hour.

Meanwhile, preheat the oven to 200 degrees F. Remove the crust from the bread and dice the bread into large pieces. Discard the crusts. Dry the bread on a baking sheet in the oven until slightly toasted, about 30 minutes.

Add the bread to the soup, stirring well to combine. Season to taste with salt and pepper, and adjust the consistency with water if necessary.

To serve, ladle the soup into warm bowls. Drizzle each with olive oil and garnish with some grated Parmesan and a basil leaf. Serve immediately, passing more cheese at the table.

cream of tomato soup
in puff pastry

SERVES
6

It was sometime around 1978 when Philippe Jeanty, now chef/owner of Bistro Jeanty in Napa Valley, was the chef at the nearby Domaine Chandon. He took excess tomato sauce and added cream and butter to make a tomato soup. (And why not? Campbell's was doing so well with theirs!) Still, Philippe wanted to make his soup different. That is when he thought of Paul Bocuse and his renowned truffle soup with pastry on top. Philippe combined the two ideas and made one of the most famous recipes of his career.

10 to 12 tablespoons (5 to 6 ounces) **unsalted butter,** divided

1 large (about ½ pound) **yellow onion,** sliced

6 garlic cloves

1½ teaspoons whole black peppercorns

1 teaspoon dried thyme leaves

1 bay leaf

¼ cup tomato paste

2½ pounds ripe tomatoes, cored and quartered

4 cups heavy cream

Salt

½ teaspoon ground white pepper

1 pound puff pastry sheets

1 egg

Melt 8 tablespoons of the butter in a large stockpot over medium-low heat. Add the onion, garlic, peppercorns, thyme, and bay leaf; cover and cook for about 5 minutes. Do not let the onion color. Add the tomato paste and lightly "toast" the tomato paste to cook out the raw flavor, then add the tomatoes and 1 cup water, if needed (use only if tomatoes are not ripe and juicy). Simmer over low heat until the tomatoes and onion are very soft and broken down, 30 to 40 minutes.

Purée by passing through a food mill (or use a blender in batches, then strain). Return the soup to the pot. Add the cream and the salt, white pepper, and 2 to 4 more tablespoons butter to taste. Bring the soup to a simmer, then remove it from the heat. Allow the soup to cool for 2 hours or overnight in the refrigerator.

Divide the soup among six 8-ounce soup cups or bowls. Roll out the puff pastry to ¼ inch thick. Cut out 6 rounds slightly larger than your cups. In a small bowl, beat together the egg with 1 tablespoon cold water. Use a brush to paint the dough with the egg wash and then turn the circles, egg wash–side down, over the tops of the cups, pulling lightly on the sides to make the dough somewhat tight like a drum. (Try not to allow the dough to touch the soup.)

Preheat the oven to 450 degrees F. Lightly paint the top of the dough rounds with egg wash without pushing the dough down. Bake until the dough is golden brown, 10 to 15 minutes. Do not open the oven in the first several minutes of cooking, as the dough may fall. Serve immediately.

chilled red pepper soup
with sumac, basil, and lemon yogurt

SERVES
6

This refreshing chilled purée from *Sunday Suppers at Lucques* by Suzanne Goin, chef/owner of Lucques Restaurant in L.A., wakes up your palate with a jolt of sweet pepper essence, cooling yogurt, and the ubiquitous Middle Eastern spice sumac. Sumac is made from the dried berries of a sumac tree, and in the Middle East it's sprinkled over everything from kabobs to yogurt to rice. The dark-crimson powder lends an acidic, lemony flavor to this soup. In a pinch, you can substitute cumin for sumac.

½ cup extra-virgin olive oil

1 small sprig fresh rosemary

1 dried chile de arbol, crumbled

2 cups diced onion

1 tablespoon fresh thyme

Kosher salt

Freshly ground black pepper

7 large red bell peppers (about 1¾ pounds)

2 teaspoons ground sumac, divided

¼ teaspoon granulated sugar

1 cup whole-milk yogurt, Greek-style if possible

1 tablespoon freshly squeezed lemon juice

2 tablespoons sliced fresh opal basil

Heat a large pot or Dutch oven over high heat for 2 minutes. Add the oil, rosemary, and chile. Let them sizzle a minute or so, and then add the onion, thyme, 1 teaspoon salt, and a good amount of black pepper. Reduce the heat to medium-high and cook, stirring often, until the onion is soft, translucent, and starting to color, about 10 minutes.

While the onion is cooking, cut the bell peppers in half lengthwise, through the stems. Use a paring knife to remove the stems, seeds, and membranes. Cut the peppers into rough 1-inch pieces.

Raise the heat back to high and add the peppers, 1 teaspoon of the sumac, the sugar, 1 teaspoon salt, and more black pepper. Sauté, stirring often with a wooden spoon, until the peppers start to caramelize slightly, about 5 minutes.

Add 8 cups water and bring to a boil. Turn the heat down to low, and simmer until the peppers are cooked through and tender but not mushy, about 30 minutes. You can test by scooping a piece of pepper onto a cutting board and pressing it with your finger or a spoon. When it's done, the flesh will give way easily.

Strain the soup over a large bowl. Put half of the peppers into a blender with ½ cup of the liquid. (You will need to purée the soup in batches.) Blend at the lowest speed until the peppers are puréed. Begin pouring in the strained liquid, a little at a time, until the soup has the consistency of heavy cream. Turn the speed to high, and blend until the soup is completely smooth, at least 1 minute. Transfer to a container, and repeat with the second half of the soup. (You may not need all the liquid.) Taste for balance and seasoning, and then chill.

While the soup is chilling, stir the yogurt, lemon juice, and ¼ teaspoon salt together in a small bowl.

When the soup is cold, serve it in chilled bowls and garnish with large dollops of lemon yogurt, a sprinkling of sumac, and the opal basil. Or, to serve family style, place the soup in a chilled tureen, garnish with the sumac and basil, and serve the lemon yogurt on the side.

cream of corn soup
with basil oil

SERVES **4** TO **6**

Drizzled with a splash of fragrant basil oil just before serving, this elegant but easy puréed soup by Linda Carucci, author of *Cooking School Secrets for Real World Cooks*, is particularly flavorful in the summertime when fresh corn is in season. It's also a comforting antidote to a cold winter day; simply substitute frozen yellow corn kernels for the fresh corn. To prevent fresh corn from spraying all over when cutting the kernels off the cob, hold the cob horizontally on the cutting board as you cut off the kernels. Or, hold the cob vertically and cut off the kernels from the bottom half first, then turn the cob so you're holding onto the cut end as you shave off the remaining kernels. Whichever way you remove the kernels, be sure to run the dull side of the knife blade down the cob to coax out the flavorful "milk." To extract even more flavor from the corn after removing the kernels, simmer the cobs with the soup, removing them before blending.

3 tablespoons unsalted butter

2 leeks, white and pale green parts only, cut into $\frac{1}{4}$ -inch rounds, swished clean in a bowl of warm water, and drained

4 cups Chicken Stock (page 13), **Vegetable Stock** (page 15), or **broth**

About 5 cups corn kernels (from 5 large ears of corn or two 16-ounce packages frozen kernel corn), divided

3 sprigs fresh thyme or **$\frac{1}{2}$ teaspoon dried thyme**

1 to 2 teaspoons salt

A few shakes Tabasco sauce

$\frac{1}{2}$ cup heavy cream

$\frac{1}{2}$ teaspoon granulated sugar (optional)

About 2 teaspoons basil oil, for serving (recipe follows)

Melt the butter in a heavy 4-quart pot over medium-high heat. When hot enough to sizzle a piece of leek, add the leeks and sauté until they become translucent, but not brown, 6 to 8 minutes. Add the stock, 4 cups of the corn kernels, the thyme, 1 teaspoon of the salt, and the Tabasco. Bring to a boil, reduce the heat, cover, and simmer until the corn is tender, about 10 minutes. Remove any thyme stems and discard.

Use a blender to purée the soup in 2 batches until creamy and smooth, holding down the blender lid as you gradually increase and decrease the speed. Strain the soup through a medium mesh sieve into a clean pot. Add the cream and reserved 1 cup corn and bring the soup to a gentle simmer over medium-high heat, stirring constantly. Reduce the heat to the lowest setting. Taste and add more salt and the sugar, if necessary, to brighten the flavor of the soup. If you'd like the corn kernels to remain crunchy, serve as is. Otherwise, continue simmering the soup until they reach the desired texture, another 5 minutes or so.

Ladle the soup into warm bowls and drizzle with the basil oil. Cool any remaining soup to room temperature before storing; cover, and refrigerate for up to 3 days.

basil oil

MAKES **1½** CUPS OIL

If you puree basil leaves in oil in your blender, then heat and strain the oil, what's left is a pure, fresh-tasting flavored oil. This recipe from *Cat Cora's Kitchen* is simple, but the basil leaves have to be perfectly fresh, and you'll want to use a very good extra-virgin olive oil.

3 cups firmly packed basil leaves
1½ cups extra-virgin olive oil

Put the basil leaves in a blender with the olive oil and process to a smooth puree.

Pour the basil-oil mixture into a saucepan over medium heat. Once the mixture simmers, let it cook for no more than 45 seconds. Pour into a chinois or fine-mesh sieve over a clean bowl. Give the oil time to drain; don't try and push it through the sieve.

If you'd like, strain the oil again through a paper coffee filter. Store the basil oil in an airtight jar, away from direct sunlight.

bean, grain, and legume soups 3

borlotti bean and vegetable soup
with pasta, pancetta, and rosemary
pasta e fagioli

SERVES
6

Janet Fletcher found culinary inspiration in Italy's rural peasant kitchens, where people have had to figure out how to make much from a little. This recipe from *Four Seasons Pasta* reflects the country's resourceful spirit: With the provisions from the pantry and a winter vegetable or two, cooks create sturdy soups that provide enormous pleasure. If you can't find borlotti beans, also known as cranberry beans, use cannellini beans.

1½ **cups dried borlotti** (cranberry) **beans,**
  soaked overnight in water to cover

3 **tablespoons extra-virgin olive oil,**
  plus more for drizzling

3 **ounces pancetta,** minced

½ **yellow onion,** minced

2 **large garlic cloves,** minced

1½ **tablespoons minced fresh rosemary**

1 **tablespoon minced fresh sage**

2 **stalks celery,** cut in ½-inch dice

12 **ounces russet** (baking) **potato,**
  peeled and cut in ½-inch dice

Salt

Freshly ground black pepper

8 **ounces small soup pasta,**
  such as ditali or tubetti

Drain the beans.

Heat the 3 tablespoons oil and the pancetta in a large pot over medium-low heat. Cook until the pancetta renders some of its fat and begins to crisp. Add the onion, garlic, rosemary, and sage. Cook until the onion is soft, about 10 minutes. Add the beans, celery, potato, and 2 quarts cold water. Bring to a simmer, stirring occasionally. Cover and adjust the heat to maintain a gentle simmer. Cook until the beans are tender, about 1 hour.

With a slotted spoon, transfer about 4 cups of the beans and vegetables to a food processor, leaving the broth in the pot. Process until smooth, adding enough broth to the food processor to make a purée. Return the purée to the pot. Stir well and season with salt and pepper to taste.

Bring the soup to a simmer over medium heat. Add the pasta, cover, and adjust the heat to maintain a gentle simmer. Cook until the pasta is barely al dente. Remove from the heat and let stand, covered, for 10 minutes before serving. Serve in warm bowls, drizzling each portion with extra-virgin olive oil.

farro and kale soup
with poached egg and parmesan crostini

SERVES
4

Elizabeth Falkner, chef/owner of Citizen Cake in San Francisco, loves to makes this soup on foggy San Francisco days, but it goes over well in warm or cold weather. Farro is an ancient grain, known for its nutritious properties. Kale is equally nutritious, and Elizabeth recommends using dinosaur, red, green, or black varieties. Topped with an egg, this soup is a healthy one-dish meal. You can make the crostini ahead of time or while the farro is cooking. You can also omit the farro for a quick and flavorful egg-drop soup.

PARMESAN CROSTINI

4 thin slices levain or **sourdough bread**

3 tablespoons olive oil

Kosher salt

4 tablespoons hand-grated Parmesan cheese, preferably Parmigiano-Reggiano

SOUP

½ cup farro or **soft wheat berries**

Kosher salt

1 quart Chicken Stock (page 13) or **broth**

2 to 4 leaves kale, stemmed and cut into chiffonade (thin ribbons)

1 garlic clove, thinly sliced

Freshly ground black pepper

Hot sauce

1 teaspoon white wine vinegar

4 eggs

Squeeze fresh lemon juice

TO MAKE THE CROSTINI, preheat the oven to 375 degrees F. Spread the slices of bread on a baking sheet and brush with the oil. Sprinkle a little salt on each slice and top with the Parmesan. Bake until the toasts are browned on the edges, about 10 minutes. Remove and set aside.

TO MAKE THE SOUP: In a small saucepan, combine the farro, 2 to 2½ cups water, and 1 teaspoon of salt and bring to a boil. Reduce the heat to low and simmer until the farro is tender, 30 to 40 minutes. Remove from the heat, drain, and set aside.

In a medium saucepan, combine the stock, kale, and garlic and bring to a boil. Reduce the heat to low and simmer for 10 minutes. Season the soup with salt and pepper to taste and a dash of hot sauce.

Fill a medium pot three-fourths full of water and bring it to a boil. Add the vinegar, then turn the heat to low until the water is at a low simmer. Carefully crack each egg into the water. (You can do 2 batches of 2.) Let the eggs poach until the whites are set but the yolks are still runny, about 3 minutes with the water barely simmering. Remove the eggs carefully with a slotted spoon and divide them among 4 soup bowls.

To finish the soup, remove some kale from the pot with a fork or tongs and place it around each egg in the soup bowls. Ladle some of the farro and soup into each bowl. Squeeze a little lemon on each serving. Serve with the crostini.

tuscan minestrone
with white beans

SERVES **6** TO **8**

This recipe from Carol Field, author of *Celebrating Italy* and *In Nonna's Kitchen,* comes from Riccardo and Gianna Bertelli, lifelong friends who Carol and her husband met when they first went to live in Italy in 1972. The two couples bonded over many things, not least of which was Riccardo and Gianna's dedication to serving traditional Tuscan dishes. Riccardo became Carol's guru on the subject of Italian food, especially the food of Tuscany, and Gianna was and still is a fabulous cook. Adding pesto, the traditional sauce of Liguria, was Carol's own touch.

SOUP

2 cups dried white beans, soaked overnight in water to cover

Sea salt

⅓ cup olive oil

1 onion, diced

2 stalks celery, diced

1 carrot, diced

2 garlic cloves, minced

2 sprigs fresh rosemary

5 teaspoons tomato paste

½ head Savoy cabbage, shredded

Small bunch kale (about 10 ounces), finely sliced

3 leeks, cleaned and finely sliced

3 zucchini, diced

Small handful fresh basil, finely chopped

2 tablespoons finely chopped fresh flat-leaf parsley

Freshly ground black pepper

1 cup fresh basil leaves (about 2 small bunches)

½ cup grated Parmigiano-Reggiano cheese

½ cup extra-virgin olive oil

2 tablespoons pine nuts or **toasted walnuts,** coarsely chopped

1½ garlic cloves, cut in half and coarsely chopped

Big pinch salt

½ teaspoon freshly ground black pepper

GARNISHES

6 to 8 slices grilled bread

Extra-virgin olive oil

Grated Parmigiano-Reggiano cheese

TO MAKE THE SOUP, drain the beans and place them in a large deep pot with water to cover, approximately 3 quarts. Bring to a boil and simmer very slowly until they are tender, 1½ to 2 hours. Add 2 or 2½ teaspoons salt when they have finished cooking and not before. Drain, reserve the cooking water, and purée half of the beans in a food processor or blender. Set them aside.

Heat the oil in a large sauté pan or large, deep pot. Add the onion, celery, carrot, garlic, and rosemary and sauté over medium-low heat until they are beginning to brown slightly, about 15 minutes. Dilute the tomato paste in a few tablespoons of warm water and stir it into the pot. Add the cabbage, kale, leeks, zucchini, basil, parsley, and the whole and puréed beans with their cooking water. Add salt and pepper to taste and a little extra hot water if the mixture gets too dense. Cook slowly until the vegetables are tender, about 30 minutes. If you need more water, just add it. While the minestrone is cooking, prepare the pesto.

TO MAKE THE PESTO, purée all the pesto ingredients in a food processor fitted with the steel blade or in a blender. (If you aren't serving the soup immediately, refrigerate the pesto in a small bowl covered with plastic wrap until ready to use.)

When you are ready to serve the soup, stir ¼ cup of the pesto into the minestrone. Serve the thick soup poured over slices of grilled bread and drizzle a thread of extra-virgin olive oil over the top. Pass grated Parmigiano-Reggiano at the table.

smoked ham, white bean, and tomato soup
with mint

SERVES
6

Joanne Weir, television host and author of *Weir Cooking* and *You Say Tomato*, loves the unlikely combination of tomatoes and mint. Add a little smoked ham to the mix and you have a soup straight out of Spain. Joanne serves this hearty soup in the winter when it's cold outside. Then again, she loves it in the fall and spring. Enjoy it anytime with a glass of robust red wine and some crusty bread.

¾ cup dried white beans (navy or cannellini)

6 parsley stems

2 sprigs fresh thyme

2 bay leaves

1 tablespoon olive oil

2 strips smoked bacon (2 ounces), cut into ¼-inch dice

1 medium yellow onion, minced

3 garlic cloves, minced

6 cups Chicken Stock (page 13) or broth

2 smoked ham hocks (about 1 pound)

1½ cups peeled, seeded, and chopped tomatoes, canned or fresh

3 tablespoons chopped fresh mint

Salt

Freshly ground black pepper

Pick over the beans and discard any damaged beans or stones. Rinse the beans. Put them in a bowl, add plenty of water to cover, and refrigerate for about 3 hours. Drain the beans and place them in a saucepan with the parsley stems, thyme, bay leaves, and cool water to cover by 2 inches. Simmer uncovered until tender, 40 to 50 minutes. Drain the beans and discard the parsley and thyme stems and bay leaves.

Heat the oil in a soup pot over medium heat. Add the bacon and onion and cook until the onion is soft, 10 minutes. Add the garlic and continue to cook 1 minute. Add the stock, ham hocks, and tomatoes and bring to a boil. Reduce the heat to low and cook until the ham just begins to fall from the bone, about 1 hour. Add the beans and continue to simmer until the ham falls easily from the bone, about 1 hour more.

Remove the ham hocks and let them cool enough to handle, about 15 minutes. Discard the skin and bones and cut the ham into ½-inch pieces. Add the ham and mint to the soup. Season to taste with salt and pepper.

Ladle the soup into bowls and serve immediately.

anytime split pea soup

SERVES
6

This soup, by Marion Cunningham from *Lost Recipes,* can be made anytime as long as you have a few ordinary vegetables, a few dried herbs, and some green split peas. This soup is so good, you won't miss the ham (which is usually called for), but you can add some scraps if you like. Serve in hot bowls, with rye bread and a green salad.

1 pound (about 2 cups) **dried green split peas**

2 stalks celery, chopped

2 carrots, chopped

¼ teaspoon dried thyme

¼ teaspoon dried marjoram

1 bay leaf, crumbled

Salt

Freshly ground black pepper

Put 8 cups cold water in a large soup pot and add the peas, celery, carrots, thyme, marjoram, and bay leaf. Cover and boil for 20 minutes. Reduce the heat and simmer until the split peas are very soft, about 30 minutes more. Purée the soup in batches in a blender or food processor until smooth. Adjust the seasoning, adding salt and pepper to taste.

spicy summer squash and yellow split pea soup

SERVES
6

The spice in this recipe by Ayla Algar, from *The San Francisco Chronicle Cookbook*, comes from a mix of turmeric, cumin, ginger, mustard, and black pepper. The split peas and squash, puréed together, create a very enticing combination. It's particularly good with coconut milk stirred in at the very last moment, but cream works too.

3/4 **cup dried yellow split peas,**
   soaked overnight in water to cover

1 teaspoon ground turmeric, divided

3 slices (each about 1/8 inch thick) **fresh ginger**

2 tablespoons clarified butter or **vegetable oil**

1 large onion, chopped

2 garlic cloves, chopped

1 teaspoon whole cumin seeds, ground

2 teaspoons whole coriander seeds, ground

3/4 **teaspoon black mustard seeds,** ground

1/3 **teaspoon freshly ground black pepper**

1/8 **teaspoon fenugreek seeds,** ground (optional)

2 large tomatoes, chopped

1 pound summer squash and crookneck squash,
   cubed

1 cup fresh cilantro leaves, divided

4 cups light Chicken Stock (page 13) or **water**

3/4 **cup coconut milk** or **cream**

Salt

Drain the split peas. Place them in a large saucepan; add ½ teaspoon of the turmeric, the ginger and 2 quarts water to the saucepan. Simmer until the peas are soft.

Heat the butter in a skillet over medium heat and cook the onion and garlic for 5 minutes. Stir in the remaining ½ teaspoon turmeric, the cumin, coriander, mustard seeds, pepper, and fenugreek (if using) and cook until lightly toasted, about 30 seconds. Add the tomatoes, squash, and ½ cup of the cilantro; cook until the squash is tender, about 15 minutes. Stir in the cooked split peas and the stock. Simmer, covered, to meld the flavors, about 30 minutes. Cool slightly and purée the soup in batches in a blender or food processor. Return it to the pan and stir in the coconut milk and salt to taste. Heat through and serve, garnished with a sprinkle of the remaining cilantro.

lentil and bacon soup

SERVES
6

This wonderful soup, by Charlie Trotter from *Charlie Trotter Cooks at Home*, goes together quickly. You can also make it with ham hocks instead of bacon. Simply cook the onions and carrots in 2 table-spoons canola oil instead of the bacon fat, and add the ham hocks with the lentils and 1 quart of stock. When the lentils are tender, remove the ham hocks from the pan and break the meat into bite-size pieces; discard the bones and skin. Add the meat to the lentils and proceed with the recipe, omitting the garnish of crispy bacon.

1 pound bacon, cut into julienne

1 cup diced yellow onions

1 cup diced carrots

1 cup green lentils

2 quarts Chicken Stock (page 13) or **broth,** divided

Salt

Freshly ground black pepper

½ cup chopped scallions

Cook three-quarters of the bacon in a large saucepan over medium heat until the fat is rendered, about 5 minutes. Add the onions and carrots and cook, stirring frequently, until the onions are translucent, 4 to 5 minutes. Drain any excess fat and add the lentils and 1 quart of the stock. Simmer over low heat until the lentils are tender, 40 to 50 minutes. Add the remaining 1 quart stock and season to taste with salt and pepper. Cook the soup over medium heat until hot, about 10 minutes.

Cook the remaining bacon in a hot sauté pan over medium-high heat until crispy, 8 to 10 minutes. Remove the bacon from the pan and drain on paper towels.

Ladle some of the soup into each bowl and sprinkle with the crispy bacon and the scallions.

black—eyed pea soup
with wilted greens

SERVES
6

The easiest way to make this soup by Michel Nischan, author of *Taste Pure and Simple,* is with leftover black-eyed peas and stewed greens. Because his mom was an excellent Southern cook, these ingredients were often handy when Michel was growing up. He loved digging with a ladle to the bottom of the pea pot for mashed peas, which he put in a saucepan. Next he skimmed some of the liquid off the top of the pot, added it to the pan, and tossed in a handful of leftover greens. Even though you may not be fortunate enough to have his mom cook in your kitchen, Michel has devised this simple recipe that goes together fast.

4 cups **Chicken Stock** (page 13),
   Vegetable Stock (page 15), or **ham hock stock**
   (if available)

8 ounces **dried black-eyed peas,** rinsed,
   soaked in cold water to cover for 2 hours,
   and drained

1 small onion, chopped

2 tablespoons molasses

Salt

Freshly ground black pepper

1 pound mixed bitter greens,
   such as mustard, arugula, and kale

In a large saucepan, combine the stock, peas, and onion. Bring to a simmer over medium-high heat. Reduce the heat to medium-low and cook, uncovered, until the peas are slightly tender but not mushy, 20 to 25 minutes.

Use a large ladle to remove about half the peas. Set these aside.

Cook the remaining peas over medium-low heat until they begin to break apart. Whisk the soup vigorously until the peas break down and create a slightly thickened soup.

Return the reserved peas to the soup. Add the molasses, and salt and pepper to taste. Return to a simmer and add the greens. Gently stir in the greens until they just begin to wilt. Taste and adjust the seasoning. Serve immediately.

fresh cranberry bean soup
with shiitake mushrooms, tofu, and chinese spinach

SERVES
6

Cranberry beans, tan with pink marbling, grow in pink-streaked pods and are also known as borlotti beans. When cooked, the pink marks disappear and their creamy texture and chestnut taste lend complex flavors to ordinary soups and simple pastas. Fresh cranberry beans are available in the summer months and can be found at farmers' markets. With the addition of tofu and sesame oil, this recipe by Alison Richman, private chef to Las Vegas mogul Steve Wynn and former chef at XYZ restaurant in San Francisco, has a slightly Asian twist.

3 tablespoons olive oil

2 onions, finely sliced

8 garlic cloves, thinly sliced

4 thin slices fresh ginger

Salt

Freshly ground black pepper

1 cup sliced fresh shiitake mushrooms

1 cup fresh or **dried cranberry beans**
(soaked overnight in water to cover if using dried)

Pinch red pepper flakes

1½ to 2 quarts Chicken Stock (page 13),
broth, or **water**

1 bunch scallions, cleaned and
sliced into 1-inch pieces

4 ounces Chinese or **regular spinach,**
roughly chopped

½ cup diced tofu (any firmness)

Sesame oil

Heat the oil in a large pot over medium heat. Add the onions, garlic, and ginger and season with salt and pepper to taste. Cover, turn the heat to low, and cook until the onions are soft, 10 to 12 minutes.

Add the mushrooms to the pot, cover, and cook until the mushrooms are soft, another 5 to 8 minutes. Add the drained dried or fresh cranberry beans and cook for 2 minutes, seasoning to taste with salt and pepper and a pinch of chile flakes. Add stock to cover the beans completely. Bring to a boil, turn the heat to low, and simmer until the beans are tender (If the beans are fresh, they'll be done in about 40 minutes; if dried, then allow for 1 to 1½ hours).

When the beans are tender, add the scallions, spinach, and tofu. Add more salt to taste, if desired. Ladle the soup into bowls, drizzle with sesame oil, and serve immediately.

spicy black bean soup

SERVES **6** TO **8**

Annie Sommerville, chef at Greens restaurant in San Francisco and author of *Fields of Greens*, created this soup as a lighter variation of her popular black bean chili. The soup is garnished here with chopped tomatoes and cilantro, but delicious possibilities abound—fried strips of corn tortilla, thinly sliced avocado, or chipotle crème fraîche.

2 cups (about 12 ounces) **dried black beans,** sorted and soaked overnight in water to cover

1 sprig fresh oregano

2 bay leaves

2 fresh sage leaves

1 tablespoon light olive oil or **vegetable oil**

1 large yellow onion, thinly sliced (about 3 cups)

½ teaspoon dried oregano, toasted in a pan for 5 minutes

Salt

Cayenne pepper

8 garlic cloves, chopped

1 heaped tablespoon ancho chiles, puréed

2 teaspoons chipotle chiles, puréed

¼ cup dry sherry

8 ounces fresh tomatoes, peeled, seeded, and chopped (about 1 cup), or **1 can** (8 ounces) **tomatoes with juice,** chopped

½ cup freshly squeezed orange juice

GARNISH

8 ounces fresh tomatoes, seeded and chopped (about 1 cup)

1 tablespoon chopped fresh cilantro

Drain and rinse the beans. Place them in a soup pot with 6 cups cold water, the oregano, and bay and sage leaves. Bring to a boil, then reduce the heat and simmer, uncovered, until the beans are soft, about 30 minutes.

Heat the oil in a sauté pan and add the onion, toasted oregano, ½ teaspoon salt, and ⅛ teaspoon cayenne. Cook over medium heat until the onion is soft, 7 to 8 minutes. Add the garlic and the chile purées. Sauté for 3 to 4 minutes, add the sherry, and simmer until it is reduced by half, a minute or two. Add the tomatoes and ½ teaspoon salt and cook for 10 minutes.

Set aside 1½ cups of the cooked beans and remove the fresh herbs and bay leaves. Combine the remaining beans and their broth with the tomatoes and onion and purée them in a blender or food processor. Pass through a food mill to remove the bean skins and return the purée to the soup pot; add the reserved beans, the orange juice, and ½ teaspoon salt. Season with salt and cayenne to taste. Cover and cook over low heat for 30 minutes.

In a small bowl, toss the tomatoes and cilantro together. Ladle the soup into bowls and garnish each serving with a spoonful of the tomato-cilantro mixture.

silky red bean soup

No one seems to really know why the tradition of red beans and rice began, but everyone knows where! Red beans and rice is an age-old ritual every Monday in New Orleans. Red kidney beans are simmered with onions, ham hocks, and bacon until they make their own flavorful, thick, natural gravy. They are served atop the favorite grain of Louisiana—rice. Often they are accompanied by andouille sausage and always lots of French bread. Everyone has their own little table treatment to personalize the concoction, but Tabasco and pepper vinegar are often included, while others insist that it must be Crystal Hot Sauce. The beloved and famous trumpeter Louis "Satchmo" Armstrong used to sign autographs "Red Beans and Ricely Yours." Jan Birnbaum, formerly chef at Catahoula in Calistoga, California, offers this recipe true to these wonderful flavors and textures, but presented in a more refined way. This makes a lot of soup, so have some friends over and have a party. If this batch is too big, you can freeze some of it for a rainy day.

5 strips bacon, diced

3 yellow onions, cut into medium dice

8 garlic cloves

1 bay leaf

½ bunch scallions, chopped green and white parts

2 tablespoons paprika

1 tablespoon ground mustard

1 tablespoons freshly ground black pepper

2 teaspoons toasted cumin seeds, ground

2 teaspoon toasted coriander seeds, ground

2 teaspoons cayenne

14 cups rich Chicken Stock (page 13) or **broth**

2 smoked ham hocks

4 ounces dried red kidney beans, soaked overnight in water to cover and drained

2 tablespoons chopped fresh thyme

½ cup red wine vinegar

3 tablespoons kosher salt

5 dashes Tabasco or other hot sauce

1½ cups cooked rice

2 tablespoons chopped fresh parsley

In a large soup pot over medium heat, render the bacon until browned. Add the onions, garlic, and bay leaf. Cook over medium heat until the onions start to brown, about 10 minutes. Add half of the scallions and cook until they soften, 5 to 8 minutes. Add the paprika, ground mustard, pepper, cumin, coriander, and cayenne. Cook for 5 minutes, scraping the bottom of the pot as you go. Add the stock, ham hocks, and beans and bring to a boil over high heat. Lower the heat and simmer for 15 to 20 minutes, skimming and discarding foam and fat that comes to the surface. Simmer, covered, until the beans are soft and creamy in the center, approximately 45 minutes more. Total cooking time is 1 hour. Add the thyme.

Remove the hocks and allow them to cool. Once they are cool enough to handle, pick the meat off of the bones in bite-size pieces. Discard the bones and save the picked meat. Strain the beans from the broth, reserving the liquid. Place the beans in a blender or food processor, working in batches if necessary. Add the vinegar, salt, and Tabasco to the beans in the blender and cover them with just enough broth to help purée the beans. Purée until smooth, then add the beans back to the simmering broth. Adjust the seasoning with salt, pepper, and Tabasco to suit your taste.

Warm a large soup terrine. Place the picked meat in the terrine and pour the hot soup over it. Garnish with the remaining sliced scallions and the rice and chopped parsley. Ladle into hot bowls to serve.

chicken, turkey, and duck
soups **4** and stews

chicken soup
with matzoh balls

Joan Nathan, author of *The New American Cooking* and *Jewish Cooking in America*, makes chicken soup in winter for the Sabbath meal, and of course, this is the first thing she thinks to make when someone in her family is sick. Matzoh balls are added for every Jewish holiday. She often makes more broth to use as a base for other soups.

1 large (3 to 5 pounds) **stewing or roasting chicken,** cut into 8 serving pieces

2 stalks celery, sliced into 2-inch chunks

2 large carrots, cut into chunks

1 large onion, quartered

1 large parsnip, cut into chunks

2 tablespoons chopped fresh dill

2 tablespoons chopped fresh parsley

Salt

Freshly ground black pepper

Matzoh Balls (optional; page 71)

Put 4 quarts water in a soup pot and bring to a boil. Add the chicken pieces. Reduce the heat to low, skimming off the foam that accumulates at the top of the soup, and cook for 2 hours, uncovered.

After 2 hours, add the celery, carrots, onion, parsnip, dill, and parsley. Continue cooking slowly, uncovered, for another hour.

Set a strainer over a large bowl and strain the soup and discard the solids. Season it to taste with salt and pepper. Refrigerate the soup, covered, overnight.

The next day, skim off the layer of solid fat that has formed on the soup's surface. Bring the soup to a boil, or freeze it for another day. Before serving, after bringing the soup to a boil, add matzoh balls (if desired), and cook for a few minutes to heat them through.

matzoh balls

MAKES **12** BALLS

1¼ cups matzoh meal

6 large eggs, well beaten

3 tablespoons chicken fat or vegetable oil

1 tablespoon chopped fresh parsley

1 teaspoon salt

1 teaspoon minced fresh ginger

¼ teaspoon ground nutmeg

In a medium bowl, mix together all the ingredients. Cover and refrigerate for a few hours or overnight.

Bring 3 quarts water to a boil in a large pot. Take the matzoh mix out of the refrigerator and, after dipping your hands into a bowl of cold water, gently form 12 balls the size of large walnuts. Add salt to the water and drop in the balls. Simmer slowly, covered, until balls are firm, about 20 minutes. Remove from the water with a slotted spoon, and add to the soup.

cream of chicken and fennel soup

SERVES
4

Rich and satisfying, this chicken soup by Betty Rosbottom, author of *The Big Book of Backyard Cooking*, gets an unexpected yet delicious infusion of flavor from fennel. Both chopped fennel bulbs and crushed fennel seeds provide a nice anise-scented touch to this extra-smooth and creamy potage. Serve this soup with some warm multigrain or whole wheat bread for a comforting lunch or supper.

2 medium **fennel bulbs**

1 quart reduced-sodium **chicken broth**
   or **Chicken Stock** (page 13)

1½ cups (about 8 ounces) **sliced baby carrots**

2 cups diced, cooked **chicken,** preferably more
   white meat than dark meat (see **NOTE**)

2½ tablespoons unsalted **butter**

2½ tablespoons **flour**

1½ cups **light cream**

2 tablespoons freshly squeezed **lemon juice**

2 teaspoons **fennel seeds,** crushed

1 teaspoon **kosher salt**

1 cup (2½ to 3 ounces) **snow peas**

3 tablespoons chopped fresh **Italian parsley**
   (optional)

Trim the lacy stalks from the fennel, reserving 4 or 5 of the lacy sprigs for the garnish if desired. Halve the bulbs lengthwise; cut out and discard the tough cores. Chop enough fennel to yield 1½ cups.

Bring the broth to a simmer in a large pot over medium-high heat. Add the fennel and carrots, and cook until the vegetables are tender when pierced with a knife, about 12 minutes.

Strain the fennel and carrots and reserve 1½ cups of the broth. (Save any extra broth for another use.) Place the fennel, carrots, and diced chicken in a large bowl.

Melt the butter in a large, heavy saucepan over medium-high heat. Add the flour and cook, stirring until golden, 1 minute or less. Gradually whisk in the cream and reserved broth until the mixture thickens slightly and coats the back of a spoon, 4 minutes or longer. Stir in the lemon juice, fennel seeds, and salt. Stir in the chicken, fennel, and carrots. (The soup can be prepared 1 day ahead; cool, cover, and refrigerate. Reheat over medium heat, stirring.)

When ready to serve the soup, trim and discard the ends from the snow peas. Cut the snow peas on the diagonal into thirds. Add the snow peas to the soup, and cook just until tender, about 2 minutes.

Ladle the soup into 4 bowls. Garnish each serving with a fennel sprig or with some chopped parsley, if desired.

NOTE: You can use your own leftover roast chicken in this recipe or buy a plain or herb-seasoned roast chicken from the grocery.

coq au vin

SERVES
8

The classic coq au vin originated in Burgundy, where it is traditionally made with a fresh chicken, aromatic bacon, juicy little mushrooms, and a bottle of wine. This stew, by Roland Passot, chef/owner of La Folie restaurant in San Francisco, is great as a weekend lunch or a hearty dinner, served with crusty bread and a crisp salad. The chicken needs to marinate overnight, so it is best to start the day before.

One 3- to 5-pound chicken, preferable free-range, cut into 8 serving pieces

Two bottles (1¼ liters) **red Burgundy** or **Beaujolais wine**

2 carrots, peeled and cut on the bias

1 onion, thinly sliced

1 tablespoon olive oil

Freshly ground black pepper

2 bay leaves

1 sprig fresh thyme

Salt

¼ cup vegetable oil

2 cups Chicken Stock (page 13) **or veal stock**

24 pearl onions, trimmed

12 tablespoons (6 ounces) **unsalted butter**

2 garlic cloves, sliced

8 ounces slab bacon, blanched and cut in ¼-inch pieces, or salted pork belly

8 ounces fresh button mushrooms, sliced

1 bunch fresh parsley, chopped

Place the chicken, wine, carrots, onion, olive oil, 1 tablespoon pepper, bay leaves, and thyme in a large bowl or pot. Cover and refrigerate overnight.

The next day, remove the chicken and vegetables from the marinade. Strain the marinade through a colander over a bowl to reserve the onion and carrots. Strain the marinade again through a fine sieve over another bowl to reserve the marinade. Discard the herbs.

Pat the chicken dry and season with salt and pepper on both sides.

In a large skillet, heat the vegetable oil. Add the chicken, a few pieces at a time, starting with the legs and thighs. Sauté until golden brown on all sides. Add the marinated onion and carrots. Transfer the chicken and vegetables to a Dutch oven or large, deep casserole.

Deglaze the skillet with the reserved marinade, then add the deglazed marinade to the chicken. Bring the mixture to a boil, then add the stock. Simmer until the chicken is tender and the sauce has thickened, 45 minutes to 1 hour.

Meanwhile, bring a medium pot of water to a boil. Drop in the pearl onions and boil for 1 minute. Drain and cool just until you can squeeze each onion out of its peel. Discard the peels.

Melt the butter in a large skillet and add the garlic, blanched bacon, pearl onions, and mushrooms. Sauté until the onions are tender, a few minutes. Add salt and pepper to taste.

Just before serving, add the vegetables on top of the chicken, and sprinkle with fresh parsley.

porcini and chicken chowder

SERVES
4

With a good, crusty baguette and a crisp, green salad, this robust chowder by Sara Perry, cookbook author and columnist for the *Oregonian*, makes a satisfying main course any time of year. The porcini mushrooms add depth and an infusion of flavor you can't quite identify, while the red pepper flakes give just the right spicy heat. In the summer, Sara uses fresh corn off the cob, herbs from the garden, and tomatoes she's oven-roasted, but in the winter, she relies on her pantry and the freezer. (By the way, she likes to use the fire-roasted canned tomatoes and frozen corn when she can find them at Trader Joe's.)

⅓ cup (2½ ounces) **dried porcini mushroom pieces**

1 quart low-sodium chicken broth, heated and divided

2 thick, smoked bacon slices (2 ounces), cut crosswise into 1-inch pieces

1 medium onion, cut into ¼-inch dice

1 boneless, skinless chicken breast half (4 to 6 ounces), diced

2 large garlic cloves, minced

1 can (28 ounces) **diced tomatoes**

1 large russet potato, peeled and cut into ¼-inch dice

1 small bay leaf

2 teaspoons dried thyme

1 teaspoon dried basil

1 teaspoon herbes de Provence (available in supermarket spice section)

Scant ½ **teaspoon red pepper flakes**

½ **teaspoon ground allspice**

Salt

1½ **cups fresh** or **frozen corn kernels**

2 cups packed baby spinach leaves, sliced into thin strips

2 tablespoons chopped fresh parsley

2 tablespoons chopped fresh cilantro

Put the mushrooms in a small bowl and cover with 1 cup of the hot broth. Set aside.

In a Dutch oven, cook the bacon pieces over medium-low heat, turning as needed to achieve uniform crispness. Using a slotted spoon, transfer the bacon to a paper towel to drain, reserving up to 2 tablespoons fat in the pot. Crumble the bacon and set aside.

In the same pot, add the onion and sauté over medium heat, stirring frequently, until soft, about 3 minutes. Add the diced chicken and cook, stirring often, until it turns white, about 4 minutes. Stir in the garlic and sauté for 1 minute. Add the remaining 3 cups broth, the tomatoes with their juice, potato, bay leaf, thyme, basil, herbes de Provence, red pepper flakes, allspice, and ½ teaspoon salt. Bring to a boil, reduce the heat to a simmer, and cook until the potatoes are just tender, 10 to 15 minutes. Add the corn and spinach and taste, adjusting the seasoning with salt. Cook until the corn is hot. Just before serving, stir in the parsley and cilantro and ladle into bowls. Garnish with the reserved bacon pieces.

sylvie's stars and moon soup

SERVES **2** TO **4**

Dana Cowin, editor in chief of *Food & Wine*, makes this soup almost every Saturday in the winter with her daughter Sylvie. The soup is named after Sylvie because it has a little bit of everything she loves: pasta, pasta, pasta, and her favorite vegetables. Don't be alarmed if the soup seems more like a stew—that's how Sylvie likes it. Feel free to take liberties: Add more chicken broth, change the vegetables, or add seasonings. It's the most forgiving and versatile dish you'll ever make.

2 cans (14.5 ounces each) **chicken broth**

2 medium carrots, peeled and cut into coins

¼ **cup orecchiette**

½ **cup elbow macaroni**

½ **cup mini pasta stars**

1 cup frozen shelled edamame

8 green beans, cut in ½-inch pieces

1 cup shredded, cooked chicken

Freshly ground black pepper

Pour the broth into a medium saucepan over medium-high heat. Add the carrots and bring to a boil. Add the orecchiette and cook for 2 minutes. Add the macaroni and cook for 3 minutes more. Add the stars, edamame, and green beans and cook for 4 minutes more. Add the chicken, cook until it is heated through, then sprinkle with pepper and serve.

chicken, turkey, and duck soups and stews

chicken stewed in
wine, garlic, and cinnamon

SERVES **4** TO **6**

This stew by Cat Cora, television host and author of *Cat Cora's Kitchen,* melds the distinctive flavors of cinnamon, onions, and garlic to make a dish inspired by her Greek heritage. As this *kota kapama* (cinnamon stewed chicken) simmers on top of your stove, it will fill your home with a heavenly fragrance. For the best flavor, use a whole bird and cut it yourself or have your butcher cut your chicken for you. For a true *kota kapama,* finish the dish with an aromatic sheep's milk cheese such as mizithra. If you can't find this, use Kasseri cheese or freshly grated Romano. Cat recommends serving this savory dish over homemade buttered noodles.

One 2½ - to 3-pound chicken, cut into
   8 serving pieces

2 teaspoons kosher salt

1 teaspoon ground cinnamon

½ teaspoon freshly ground black pepper

5 garlic cloves, divided

2 tablespoons extra-virgin olive oil

4 cups coarsely chopped yellow onions

½ cup dry white wine

1 can (6 ounces) tomato paste

½ cup grated mizithra, Kasseri, or Romano cheese

Pat the chicken pieces dry with paper towels so they don't spatter in the pan. Mix the salt, cinnamon, and pepper together in a small bowl and rub the chicken pieces on all sides with the mixture. Mince 3 of the garlic cloves and set aside.

Heat the oil in a large, deep, nonaluminum skillet over high heat. (A 12-inch skillet with sides about 3 inches high will allow you to brown all the chicken pieces at once.) If you don't have a skillet large enough, brown the chicken in 2 batches, using 1 tablespoon of oil for each batch. Don't crowd the pieces in the pan or the chicken will steam rather than brown.

Add the chicken to the skillet and brown for 4 to 5 minutes on each side, shifting the pieces with a metal spatula so the chicken doesn't stick to the skillet. When the pieces are nicely browned on all sides, remove them from the pan and set aside.

Reduce the heat to medium-high and add the onions and minced garlic. Cook, stirring constantly, until the onions have softened and are rich golden brown, about 3 minutes. Add the wine and scrape the bottom of the pan with a spatula or spoon to deglaze, loosening any browned bits.

When the wine has evaporated, add 2 cups water, the tomato paste, and the remaining 2 whole garlic cloves. Return the chicken to the pan. The liquid should cover about three-quarters of the chicken. Reduce the heat to low, cover the skillet with a lid, and simmer until the chicken is tender and thoroughly cooked, about 1 hour. (If the sauce becomes too thick, thin it with more water.) Taste and adjust the seasoning. Sprinkle grated cheese over the top of each serving.

spring tagine of chicken
with potatoes and peas

SERVES 6 TO 8

A tagine is the quintessential Moroccan stew. The word *tagine* also refers to the unique vessel capped with a distinctive conical lid in which the food is cooked and served. Tagines are available in many cookware and import stores (although you can easily substitute a heavy Dutch oven or a slow cooker). This home-style tagine from Kitty Morse, author of *Cooking at the Kasbah*, often appears on Moroccan tables when fresh peas are in season.

2 tablespoons olive oil

2 pounds (about 8) **boneless, skinless chicken thighs**

2 pounds small, **new potatoes,** peeled

2 medium **onions,** diced

½ **bunch fresh cilantro,** rinsed and tied with string

½ **bunch fresh parsley,** rinsed and tied with string, plus **chopped fresh parsley,** for garnish

1 cup **Chicken Stock** (page 13) or **broth**

3 **garlic cloves,** minced

1 teaspoon ground turmeric

1 teaspoon ground ginger

1 teaspoon freshly ground black pepper

2 cups frozen petite peas

½ **lemon,** juiced

1½ teaspoons salt

Preheat the oven to 400 degrees F. In a tagine dish or a medium Dutch oven, heat the oil, and brown the chicken on all sides. Add the potatoes, onions, cilantro, parsley, stock, garlic, turmeric, ginger, and pepper. Cover tightly and bake until the chicken and potatoes are tender, 50 to 55 minutes. Discard the cilantro and parsley. Add the peas, lemon juice, and salt, and heat through. Garnish with chopped parsley and serve.

winter vegetable
and roast turkey chowder

SERVES
8

When Thanksgiving leftovers beckon and another turkey sandwich seems boring, reach for the soup pot and whip up a hearty and soulful bowl of turkey chowder by Diane Morgan, author of *The Thanksgiving Table*. If you like to make soups that are chock-full of vegetables, this recipe is for you. Diane recommends walking the produce aisles to see which vegetables look fresh. Butternut squash is always firm and plentiful in winter as is Swiss chard, with either red or pale white ribs. Red potatoes and onions are usually stacked high. Though zucchini is overly abundant in summer, it's in the market year-round and a great last-minute addition to the pot, so its color stays bright green.

3 slices bacon, diced

1 large yellow onion, cut into $\frac{1}{2}$-inch dice

2 large stalks celery, cut into $\frac{1}{2}$-inch dice

2 large red potatoes (about 8 ounces each), peeled and cut into $\frac{1}{2}$-inch dice

1 small butternut squash (about 1 pound), peeled, halved lengthwise, seeded, and cut into $\frac{1}{2}$-inch dice

7 cups canned low-sodium chicken broth

2 cups chopped, deribbed Swiss chard leaves

2 cups $\frac{1}{2}$-inch dice roast turkey

1 medium zucchini, cut into $\frac{1}{2}$-inch dice

2 tablespoons minced fresh flat-leaf parsley

1 tablespoon minced fresh thyme

Salt

Freshly ground black pepper

In a heavy 6- to 8-quart saucepan, cook the bacon over medium heat, stirring frequently, until browned. Remove it with a slotted spoon to a plate. Set aside. Pour off all but 2 tablespoons of the bacon fat, and return the pot to medium heat. Add the onion and celery. Sauté until the vegetables are soft but not browned, 3 to 5 minutes.

Add the potatoes, squash, and broth. Bring to a boil and reduce the heat to a simmer. Partially cover the pot and cook until the potatoes are tender, about 15 minutes. Add the chard, turkey, zucchini, parsley, thyme, and reserved bacon. Cook 5 minutes longer. Add salt and pepper to taste. Ladle the soup into warmed bowls or mugs to serve.

chicken and black bean chili
with corn, avocado, and chipotle

SERVES **6** TO **8**

On a cold day nothing will warm you, your family, and your home better than a big pot of this killer chili! This Mexican-inspired recipe by Joey Altman, the Emmy Award–winning TV host of *Bay Café*, goes together fast. The recipe calls for chipotle chiles and Mexican *cotija* cheese, both of which are available in the Latin foods section of many grocery stores. Serve with warm cornbread or tortillas.

½ cup olive or **vegetable oil,** divided

1½ pounds boneless, skinless chicken thighs, cut in 1-inch cubes

2 to 3 tablespoons chili powder

1 tablespoon cumin seeds

2 cups diced yellow onions

1 cup seeded, diced poblano chiles

1 red bell pepper, diced

3 canned chipotle chiles in adobo sauce, minced

¼ cup minced garlic (4 to 6 cloves)

1 can (14½ ounces) **black beans**

1 can (15 ounces) **diced tomatoes**

2 ears corn, kernels cut from the cobs

Salt

Freshly ground black pepper

1 ripe avocado, halved, pitted, and diced

1 cup cherry tomatoes, quartered

½ **red onion,** diced (about ½ cup)

½ **bunch fresh cilantro,** minced

½ **cup freshly squeezed lime juice** (about 4 limes)

2 jalapeño chiles, seeded and minced

1½ teaspoons kosher salt

½ **cup crumbled Mexican *cotija* cheese**

½ **cup grated mixed Cheddar and Monterey Jack cheeses**

Heat ¼ cup of the oil in a heavy-bottomed, 8-quart pot over medium heat. Add the chicken, chili powder, and cumin seeds and sauté until the chicken is cooked through, 4 to 6 minutes. Transfer the meat to a bowl and set aside.

Return the pot to the heat, add the remaining ¼ cup of oil, and cook the onions, poblanos, bell pepper, chipotles, and garlic, stirring frequently, until the onions start to brown. Stir in the beans with their liquid, tomatoes, and corn and return the cooked chicken with all its juices. Turn the heat down to low and simmer, stirring every 5 minutes, until the chicken is cooked through and tender, about 25 minutes. Season with salt and pepper to taste.

In a large bowl, combine the avocado, tomatoes, onion, cilantro, lime juice, jalapeños, and salt. Set aside.

To serve, ladle the chili into bowls and top with the salsa and cheeses.

chicken and andouille gumbo

Gumbo, redolent of smoky sausage and dark roux, is the best-known Cajun and Creole dish. This spicy stew by Bruce Aidells, from *Bruce Aidells' Complete Sausage Book*, is best made one or two days ahead so the flavors can mellow.

One 3½-pound chicken

1 onion, unpeeled and halved, plus **3 cups chopped onions**

1 carrot, cut into 2 pieces

1 stalk celery, plus **1 cup chopped celery**

1 bay leaf

1 cup peanut oil

1 cup all-purpose flour

1 green bell pepper, chopped into ¼-inch pieces

1 red bell pepper, chopped into ¼-inch pieces

1¼ pounds Cajun-style andouille or **other spicy smoked sausage;** ¼ pound chopped into ¼-inch pieces, 1 pound sliced into ¼-inch rounds

2 tablespoons minced garlic

1 teaspoon dried thyme

1 teaspoon ground cayenne

1 teaspoon freshly ground black pepper

¼ teaspoon dried sage

1 pound okra, cut into ½-inch slices

1 cup thinly sliced green onions or **scallions**

Salt

Tabasco sauce

3 cups cooked rice

½ cup chopped fresh parsley

Put the whole chicken and 2 quarts water in a large pot and bring to a boil. Skim any froth from the surface, then decrease the heat to a simmer, and add the halved onion, carrot, celery stalk, and bay leaf. Simmer until the chicken is fully cooked, about 40 minutes. Remove the chicken to cool. Strain the stock, discard the vegetables, then return the stock to the pot and continue to simmer it while you prepare the rest of the recipe.

In a heavy 3- to 4-quart pot or Dutch oven, heat the oil over medium heat for 5 minutes. Remove the pot from the heat and gradually stir in the flour. Return the pot to the heat and cook, continuing to stir, until the roux is a deep brown color, about 20 minutes. Remove the pot from the heat and add the chopped onions and celery. The vegetables will cool the roux. Return the pot to medium heat, stirring the vegetables until they are soft, about 5 minutes. The roux will continue to darken. Add the bell peppers and the ¼ pound chopped andouille and cook for 5 more minutes. Add the garlic, thyme, cayenne, pepper, and sage.

Measure the chicken stock that has been simmering. You should have 6 cups (add water if necessary). Stir the stock into the pot of vegetables, mixing well. Bring to a boil, then simmer for 15 minutes, uncovered. Add the okra and simmer for 30 minutes. While the gumbo simmers, remove the chicken meat from the bones. Discard the skin and bones, and cut the meat into ¾-inch pieces. (The gumbo and chicken can be refrigerated overnight at this point.)

If you have refrigerated the gumbo overnight, gradually bring it to a simmer. Add the sliced andouille to the simmering gumbo and cook for 10 minutes. Add the chicken meat and green onions, and simmer for 5 minutes more. Taste and adjust the seasonings with salt and Tabasco.

To serve, spoon about ½ cup warm, cooked rice into a large soup bowl. Ladle gumbo over the rice and garnish with parsley.

brazilian chicken soup

This chicken soup or *canja*, as it is called in Portuguese, is the Brazilian grandmother's cure-all. This recipe, by cookbook author and historian Jessica Harris, is adapted from her book *Tasting Brazil*.

Half a 3- to 4-pound chicken

4 medium, ripe tomatoes, peeled, seeded, and coarsely chopped

1 medium onion, chopped

1 stalk celery with leaves, chopped (including 1½ tablespoons leaves)

1 sprig fresh parsley, minced

3 large carrots, thinly sliced

½ cup uncooked white rice

Salt

Freshly ground black pepper

Place the chicken, tomatoes, onion, celery, and parsley into a large stockpot. Add 2 quarts water, cover, and bring to a boil. Reduce the heat to low and cook until the broth is flavorful, about 1 hour. Remove the soup from the heat.

Remove the chicken from the stock and let it cool. When it is cool enough to handle, strip the meat from the bones. Set the meat aside and discard the bones and skin.

Put the cooking liquid and vegetables through a food mill (or you can use an immersion blender) to obtain a thick, rich chicken stock. Return the stock to the pot, add the reserved chicken meat, carrots, rice, and 2 cups water to the pot. Place it on medium heat and bring it to a boil. Reduce the heat to low and let it simmer for an additional 30 minutes, or a bit longer if you like mushy rice. Season with salt and pepper to taste and serve hot.

asian noodle soup
with roasted duck

SERVES
4

If you have a basic homemade chicken broth in your freezer and can pick up a roasted duck or chicken from the market, this recipe—a very loose variation on the classic Vietnamese soup *pho ga*—doesn't get any easier. Writer Sara Deseran, author of *Asian Vegetables*, likes to use the good-quality egg noodles you can find in Chinese markets, although thin rice noodles are more traditional. Serve with Vietnamese chile sauce on the side.

2 tablespoons canola oil

¼ cup finely chopped shallot

5½ cups **Chicken Stock** (page 13) or **broth**

1½-inch piece fresh ginger, bruised

2 star anise

½ cinnamon stick

1 tablespoon fish sauce

Kosher salt

12 ounces fresh Chinese egg noodles

½ **roasted duck or chicken,** skin removed and meat shredded

Thai basil leaves, for garnish

Sliced jalapeño chiles, for garnish

Bean sprouts, for garnish

In a large pot over medium-high heat, warm the oil. Add the shallot and sauté until fragrant, about 15 seconds. Add the stock, bring to a simmer, and reduce the heat to low. Add the ginger, star anise, and cinnamon stick, then cover and simmer to infuse the broth with the spices, about 30 minutes. Add the fish sauce and salt to taste.

Meanwhile, bring a large pot of water to a boil. Add the noodles and cook until just tender, 2 to 3 minutes. Drain and set aside.

To the stock, add the shredded duck and simmer until heated through. Divide the noodles between 4 bowls and ladle the soup over the noodles. Serve immediately, along with a platter of Thai basil, jalapeños, and bean sprouts for garnishing.

thai-style chicken-coconut soup
with lemongrass and galanga

SERVES 4 WITH RICE AND OTHER DISHES, OR 2 AS A MAINCOURSE

Nancie McDermott, author of *Real Thai* and
Quick & Easy Vietnamese Cooking, first
encountered this soup while working as a Peace
Corps volunteer in Thailand. Most of the Asian
ingredients in this soup, such as unsweetened
coconut milk and fish sauce, can now be found
in major supermarkets. Whole Foods markets
carry fresh lemongrass, galanga, and wild lime
leaves, and you can also order them through
www.importfood.com or www.templeofthai.com.
You can also check at Asian markets in your area.
If you can't find galanga, you can use its cousin,
fresh ginger, in its place. If you can't obtain wild
lime leaves, simply leave them out. If you like a
little heat, garnish your soup with 8 to 10 tiny
green and red Thai chiles, which you have
stemmed and bruised lightly by pressing them with
the side of a large knife.

2 stalks fresh lemongrass

2 **green onions,** thinly sliced crosswise

2 **tablespoons freshly squeezed lime** or **lemon juice**

2 **tablespoons fish sauce**

6 **fresh** or **frozen wild lime leaves,**
    torn or cut into quarters, divided

10 to 12 **slices fresh, frozen,** or **dried galanga**

1 **boneless chicken breast,** cut into bite-size chunks
    or sliced crosswise into thin strips

4 **ounces fresh mushrooms,** thinly sliced
    (about 1 cup)

1 **can** (14 ounces) **unsweetened coconut milk**

1 **can** (14 ounces) **chicken broth** or **about
    2 cups Chicken Stock** (page 13)

2 **tablespoons chopped fresh cilantro**

Trim away and discard the root end and top 3 inches of each stalk of lemongrass, along with any dry outer leaves. Pound each stalk lightly with the spine of a cleaver or an unopened can. Cut each stalk crosswise into 2-inch lengths and set aside.

In a large serving bowl, combine the green onions, lime juice, fish sauce, and half of the lime leaves. Set the bowl by the stove along with small separate dishes containing the galanga, lemongrass, chicken, mushrooms, and remaining lime leaves.

In a medium saucepan, combine the coconut milk and broth. Bring to a gentle boil over medium-high heat. Stir in the galanga, lemongrass, and small dish of lime leaves. Add the chicken and mushrooms and stir well. Return to a gentle boil, reduce the heat, and simmer to infuse the flavor and cook the chicken, about 10 minutes.

Remove the pan from the heat, pour the hot soup over the herbs and seasonings in the serving bowl, and stir well. Sprinkle with the chopped cilantro and serve hot.

meaty soups 5 and stews

beef, barley, and mushroom soup

SERVES
8

Old-fashioned beef-barley soup is a traditional cool weather soup and this rustic version by Diane Rossen Worthington, from her book *Seriously Simple*, calls for meaty beef shanks to complete the meal. Two types of mushrooms—shiitake and button—and a little soy sauce add to the meaty flavor. The soup can be made up to three days in advance and should be refrigerated at least overnight to remove any fat. If you prefer a lighter soup, you can substitute chicken thighs (on the bone) for the beef shanks.

1 ounce dried shiitake mushrooms, soaked in 2 cups boiling water for 30 minutes

2 tablespoons olive oil

3 leeks, white and light green parts only, thoroughly cleaned and coarsely chopped

2 beef shanks (about 1½ pounds)

Salt

Freshly ground black pepper

2 carrots, coarsely chopped

1 pound fresh white button mushrooms, coarsely chopped

½ cup pearl barley (not quick cooking)

7 cups Chicken Stock (page 13) or **Beef Stock** (page 13) or **broth**

3 tablespoons finely chopped fresh parsley

1 tablespoon soy sauce

Strain the soaked dried mushrooms over a bowl, squeeze them dry, and reserve 1 cup of the soaking liquid. Cut the mushrooms into ¼-inch dice and put them in a small bowl. Strain the reserved mushroom liquid through a fine-mesh sieve over the mushrooms. Set aside.

In a large soup pot, heat the oil over medium-high heat. Add the leeks and sauté until they are nicely softened, stirring, 5 to 7 minutes. Season the beef shanks with salt and pepper and add to the leek mixture. Brown them on each side for about 2 minutes. Add the carrots, fresh mushrooms, and barley and sauté until coated, about 1 minute. Add the stock, reduce the heat to low, cover, and simmer the soup until the barley is tender but not mushy, 1 to 1½ hours.

Remove the beef and let it cool. Shred the meat and return it to the soup. Add the reserved dried mushrooms and liquid to the soup. Add the parsley and soy sauce and simmer until slightly thickened, about 5 minutes. Season with salt and pepper to taste. Serve immediately.

lamb stew

with mushrooms and sweet peppers from the Madonie

agnello al forno alla madonita

SERVES
6

The Madonie is a mountain range in northern Sicily between the towns of Cefalu and Enna. This recipe by Joyce Goldstein, from her book *Italian Slow and Savory,* is a bit unusual for the cooks in the region, who usually prefer oregano over rosemary and who would rather add either peppers or mushrooms, but not both. Serve this with roast or mashed potatoes.

3 pounds boneless lamb shoulder, trimmed of excess fat and cut into 2-inch pieces

About 1 cup olive oil, divided

4 garlic cloves, smashed, **plus 2 cloves,** minced

¼ cup freshly squeezed lemon juice, plus more to taste

2 tablespoons chopped fresh rosemary or **2 teaspoons dried oregano**

3 yellow onions, thickly sliced

½ cup dry white wine

3 red or **yellow bell peppers** cut lengthwise into wide strips

1½ pounds large, fresh brown mushrooms, such as porcini or portobello, wiped clean and quartered

Salt

Freshly ground black pepper

In a large bowl, toss together the lamb, ½ cup of the oil, the smashed garlic, ¼ cup lemon juice, and rosemary. Cover and refrigerate a few hours or for as long as overnight.

Preheat the oven to 400 degrees F. Remove the lamb from the marinade and place it in a Dutch oven or a baking dish with a lid. Reserve the garlic and bits of herbs from the marinade.

In a large sauté pan, heat 2 or 3 tablespoons of oil over medium heat. Add the onions and sauté until softened, about 10 minutes. Add the onions to the lamb along with the wine and reserved garlic and herbs and mix well. Cover tightly and bake for 45 minutes. While the lamb is cooking, return the sauté pan to medium heat and add 2 tablespoons of oil. Add the bell pepper strips and sauté until tender, about 8 minutes. Using a slotted spoon, transfer the pepper strips to a plate.

Return the pan to medium heat and add 2 or 3 tablespoons oil. Add the mushrooms and sauté until softened, about 5 minutes. Stir in the minced garlic and cook for 1 to 2 minutes.

Remove the lamb from the oven and reduce the oven temperature to 325 degrees F. Add the sautéed peppers and mushrooms to the lamb, then re-cover and return it to the oven. Continue to cook until the lamb is tender, about 1 hour longer.

Remove the lamb from the oven and season to taste with salt, pepper, and lemon juice. Serve at once.

moroccan lamb and garbanzo soup

SERVES **6** TO **8**

Rick Rodgers, author of *The Carefree Cook*, adjusted one of his favorite soups, rich with Moroccan spices, to use readily available supermarket lamb chops. If you wish, season it with *harissa*, a Moroccan chile paste available at specialty food stores, after cooking. And pass plenty of warm pita bread.

1 teaspoon coriander seeds

1 teaspoon cumin seeds

¼ teaspoon ground cinnamon

¼ teaspoon red pepper flakes

3 lamb shoulder chops, cut about ¾ inch thick (about 12 ounces each)

3 tablespoons olive oil, divided

1 medium onion, chopped

2 large garlic cloves, finely chopped

2 cups Chicken Stock (page 13) or **broth**

1 can (28 ounces) **diced tomatoes in juice**

1 can (15 to 19 ounces) **garbanzo beans** (chickpeas), drained and rinsed

Salt

Chopped fresh cilantro or **mint,** for garnish

Heat a small skillet over medium-high heat. Add the coriander and cumin seeds and cook, stirring occasionally, until toasted and fragrant. Transfer the seeds to a mortar or spice grinder and crush into a coarse powder. Add the cinnamon and pepper flakes and mix well. (You can also put the seeds on a work surface and crush under a heavy saucepan.) Set the spice mixture aside.

Cut the meat from the bones, trimming away any excess fat, and cut it into bite-size pieces. Reserve the meat and bones, and discard the fat and trimmings.

Heat 1 tablespoon of the oil in a large soup pot over medium-high heat. In batches without crowding, add the lamb pieces and bones and cook, stirring occasionally, until browned, about 4 minutes. Using a slotted spoon, transfer them to a bowl.

Add the remaining 2 tablespoons of the oil to the pot and reduce the heat to medium. Add the onion and cook until softened, about 3 minutes. Stir in the garlic and cook until it softens, about 1 minute. Add the spice mixture and stir until it gives off its aroma, about 15 seconds. Add the stock and stir up the browned bits in the pot. Return the lamb bones, meat, and juices to the pot. Stir in the tomatoes and their juice and 2 cups water. Bring to a boil over high heat, skimming off any foam that rises to the surface. Reduce the heat to medium-low and simmer, uncovered, until the lamb is tender, about 1 hour. Add the beans and cook until heated through, about 10 minutes. Season with salt to taste. Remove the lamb bones. Discard them, or nibble the meat off the bones as the cook's treat.

Serve hot in soup bowls, garnished with the cilantro.

spicy lamb soup
with cinnamon, orzo, lemon, and dates

Leslie's mother, Suzanne Jonath, found inspiration for this soup after her travels to North Africa. This soup, adapted from the Time-Life series book on Morocco, is traditionally made during Ramadan. The lemony flavor of the soup is nicely balanced with a hint of cinnamon and the sweet touch of dates.

2 to 3 tablespoons olive oil

12 ounces lean, boneless lamb shoulder, trimmed of excess fat, sliced $1/8$ inch thick, and cut into 1-x-$1/8$-inch strips

1 teaspoon ginger

$1/3$ teaspoon turmeric

4 ripe tomatoes, peeled, seeded, and cut into 1-inch chunks

1 yellow onion, diced

3 to 4 tablespoons finely chopped fresh cilantro, plus extra for garnish

2 teaspoons salt

$3/4$ teaspoon freshly ground black pepper

$1/2$ cup orzo

3 eggs, slightly beaten

1 tablespoon freshly squeezed lemon juice

Ground cinnamon

About 1 cup chopped dates

In a heavy Dutch oven, warm the oil over high heat until it begins to smoke. Brown the lamb evenly until richly colored. Stir in the ginger and turmeric, then add 6 cups cold water, the tomatoes, onion, cilantro, salt, and pepper. Bring to a boil, reduce the heat to low, and simmer, partially covered, for 45 minutes.

Raise the heat to high and when the soup comes to a boil, stir in the orzo. Cook, uncovered over medium heat, stirring occasionally, until the orzo is tender, about 10 minutes. Then remove the casserole from the heat and stir in the eggs, lemon juice, and a sprinkling of cinnamon. (The eggs will separate into strands). Taste for salt, pepper, and lemon juice and adjust the seasonings. Ladle into soup bowls, and garnish with fresh cilantro and dates.

drunken beef stew

Vanessa Dina, Kristina Fuller, and Gemma DePalma founded The Meat Club for women who want to have their meat and eat it too. This recipe, from *The Meat Club Cookbook*, came to them from their French friend France, who incidentally comes from France. This cold-weather meal gets better the longer it sits. This recipe calls for two types of stewing meat for richer flavor—the classic stewing meat from the chuck and the famously tender top sirloin. Let your butcher know so he can cube your pieces in advance.

3 tablespoons (1½ ounces) **unsalted butter**

8 ounces bacon

2½ **pounds top sirloin,** cut into 1-inch pieces

2½ **pounds chuck,** cut into 1-inch pieces

1 tablespoon flour

One bottle (750-milliliter) **Pinot Noir** or Burgundy wine

10 **carrots,** chopped into 1½ -inch pieces

12 pearl onions

1 **garlic clove,** minced

1½ teaspoons dried thyme

2 bay leaves

Salt

Freshly ground black pepper

Melt the butter in a large cast-iron casserole over medium heat. Add the bacon and brown until softened but not crispy, about 5 minutes. Remove the bacon and save for another use.

In the same pan, cook the meat in batches until browned evenly, 4 to 5 minutes per side. Once browned, return all the meat to the pan and sprinkle the flour over it. Mix well. Add the wine to cover the meat. Stir in the carrots, onions, garlic, thyme, and bay leaves.

Cover and cook over low to medium heat until the meat is tender enough to cut with a fork, about 2 hours. Add salt and pepper to taste.

mrs. birdsong's beef and cabbage soup
with lima beans

All small-town cooks have their claim to fame and Mrs. Birdsong Corpening—the mother of twins Mary Corpening Barber and Sara Corpening Whiteford, authors of *The Bride & Groom First and Forever Cookbook*—earned her culinary reputation with this soup. She always roasts prime-rib bones (leftovers from Christmas Eve dinner), but they have adapted the recipe to suit our time-challenged lifestyles. To enrich the flavor, they've added some chopped garlic, and serve the soup with a dash of Tabasco and a dollop of sour cream. Though the folks back in High Point, North Carolina, know and love Mrs. Birdsong's all-day-in-the-kitchen cabbage soup, thickened with slightly sweet gingersnaps, their friends in San Francisco rave about this sweet-and-sour rendition. Who says you have to roast bones to make soup that rates two thumbs up? This soup is best made at least one day in advance. It will keep, refrigerated, for several days and freezes beautifully. Allow the flavors to marry in the refrigerator for one day before freezing.

3 tablespoons **vegetable oil**, divided

1³/₄ pounds **chuck stew meat**, trimmed and cut into ¹/₂-inch pieces

1 teaspoon **kosher salt**, divided, plus more as needed

¹/₂ teaspoon **freshly ground black pepper**, divided, plus more as needed

2 small **yellow onions**, thinly sliced

2 **carrots**, roughly chopped

2 **parsnips**, roughly chopped

4 large **garlic cloves**, roughly chopped

4 cans (14 ounces each) **beef broth** (not double strength) or **7 cups Beef Stock** (page 13)

1 can (28 ounces) **crushed tomatoes** (not in purée)

4 cups roughly chopped **green cabbage**

1 package (10 ounces) **frozen butter beans** or **baby limas**

8 **gingersnaps**, finely crushed in food processor (scant ¹/₂ cup)

3 tablespoons **freshly squeezed lemon juice**, plus more as needed

3 tablespoons firmly packed **dark brown sugar**, plus more as needed

1 **bay leaf**

Tabasco sauce, for serving

Sour cream, for serving

Heat 1 tablespoon of the oil in an 8-quart, heavy-bottomed stockpot over medium-high heat. Season the meat with ½ teaspoon of the salt and ¼ teaspoon of the pepper. Add the meat and cook until browned, 3 to 5 minutes. Transfer the meat to a large plate.

Add the remaining 2 tablespoons oil to the pot. Add the onions, carrots, parsnips, the remaining ½ teaspoon salt, and the remaining ¼ teaspoon pepper. Cook, stirring occasionally, until the vegetables begin to caramelize, about 5 minutes. Add the garlic and cook, stirring constantly, for 1 minute. Add the broth and the beef, 1 quart water, the tomatoes, cabbage, butter beans, gingersnaps, lemon juice, sugar, and bay leaf. Whisk vigorously to dissolve the gingersnaps. (They may clump at first, but will disintegrate as you stir.) Bring to a boil, then reduce the heat to low. Skim the surface with a ladle to remove excess foam. Simmer, stirring occasionally, until the beef is fall-apart tender and the flavors have melded, about 1½ hours.

Season the soup with more salt, lemon juice, and sugar, if necessary. Remove the bay leaf. Ladle into bowls and top each with a dash of Tabasco sauce and a dollop of sour cream.

NOTE: This makes an extra-large pot of soup. Eat what you can and freeze the rest for later.

texas chili soup

This chili comes from Frankie's mom, JoAnn Tatum. Hot and spicy, it has kept JoAnn and her husband, John, warm many a cold winter day in east Texas. Frankie adds a dash of Tabasco to give it even more kick.

2 tablespoons (1 ounce) **unsalted butter**

1 cup chopped onion

4 teaspoons minced garlic

1 pound ground pork

1 pound ground beef or **turkey**

2 cans (29 ounces each) **diced tomatoes**

3 cans (15 to 16 ounces each) **pinto beans,**
 drained and rinsed

1 quart Beef Stock (page 13),
 Chicken Stock (page 13), or **broth**

4 stalks celery, chopped

2 tablespoons chili powder

1 tablespoon red pepper flakes

1 teaspoon cayenne pepper

1 teaspoon salt

**Shredded Cheddar and Monterey Jack
 cheeses,** for garnish

2 green onions, chopped

8 ounces sour cream

In a large pot, warm the butter over low heat and sauté the onion and garlic until golden. Add the ground pork and beef and cook until browned. Drain off half of the fat. Add the tomatoes, beans, stock, celery, chili powder, pepper flakes, cayenne, and salt and simmer until the flavors meld, 30 minutes to 1 hour.

Serve in bowls sprinkled with cheese, chopped green onions, and a dollop of sour cream.

grandma salazar's albóndigas soup

SERVES **6** TO **8**

Albóndigas is the Spanish word for meatballs. Traci des Jardins, chef/owner of Jardiniere and Mijita restaurants in San Francisco, learned to make this soup with her Mexican-born grandmother. Grandma Salazar loved to spend time with Traci in the kitchen, and called her *mijita*, meaning "little one." Traci now serves this soup at her restaurant Mijita, where she re-creates the authentic Mexican food of her childhood. This recipe calls for Mexican oregano (which has a slightly smoky flavor), but any oregano will do.

½ **cup short-grain white rice**

4 **tablespoons vegetable oil,** divided

2 **white onions,** diced

8 **ounces ground pork**

8 **ounces ground beef**

2 **eggs**

1 **bunch fresh cilantro,** picked and chopped

3 **sprigs fresh mint,** chopped

1 **tablespoon dried oregano** (preferably Mexican)

1 **teaspoon ground cumin**

1 **tablespoon salt**

½ **teaspoon freshly ground black pepper**

2 **stalks celery,** sliced

1 **carrot,** peeled and diced

1 **garlic clove,** minced

8 **ounces tomatoes,** blanched, peeled, and diced or
   1 **can** (12 ounces) **peeled and crushed tomatoes**

1 to 1½ **quarts Chicken Stock** (page 13) or **broth**

1 **zucchini,** diced

In a small pot over high heat, bring to a boil 1 cup water and pour it over the rice. Let it soak for 20 minutes and drain.

In a sauté pan, heat 2 tablespoons of the oil over medium heat and sauté half of the onions until soft. Remove from the heat and let cool.

In a large bowl, combine the cooked onion with the pork and beef. Add the soaked rice, eggs, half of the cilantro, half of the mint, the oregano, cumin, salt, and pepper. Blend together well and form into 1-inch meatballs.

In a large sauté pan over medium-high heat, add the remaining 2 tablespoons of oil and brown the meatballs lightly. Remove them from the pan and add the remaining onions, the celery, carrot, and garlic; sweat the mixture slightly and add the tomatoes. Add the stock and bring to a simmer, then add the meatballs and the remaining mint. Simmer until the flavors have melded and the meatballs are firm (but not so long that they fall apart), about 1 hour. Season to taste with salt and pepper, add the zucchini, and cook for another 10 minutes. Garnish servings with the remaining cilantro.

mexican minestrone
with chorizo

SERVES **4** TO **6**

Minestrone is an Italian word meaning "big soup," but it can easily cross cultures to describe this spicy sausage, bean, and vegetable version created by television host Tori Ritchie, author of *Braises and Stews* and *Party Appetizers*. Be sure to use fresh Mexican chorizo, not the dried Spanish variety. The perfect dipper would be corn tortillas that have been brushed with oil and sprinkled with salt and chili powder, then baked until crispy.

2 tablespoons olive oil

1 small yellow onion, chopped

1 large carrot, chopped

12 ounces Mexican chorizo

¼ cup chopped fresh cilantro

6 cups Chicken Stock (page 13) or **broth**

1 can (15 ounces) **garbanzo beans**, drained and rinsed

8 ounces ripe tomatoes, peeled, seeded, and chopped

8 ounces chayote squash or zucchini, diced

6 ounces baby spinach leaves, washed well

GARNISHES

2 limes, cut into wedges

1 bunch radishes, sliced or chopped

2 large avocados, diced

In a soup pot or Dutch oven, warm the oil over medium-high heat with the onion and carrot. Cook, stirring often, until the vegetables soften, about 3 minutes. Crumble in the chorizo, discarding the casings, and cook, breaking up the sausage with a wooden spoon, until the meat is no longer pink; drain off the fat if desired. Stir in the cilantro, then add the stock, garbanzo beans, and tomatoes. Bring to a boil, then reduce the heat, cover, and simmer for 15 minutes.

Stir in the squash and continue cooking, covered, for 5 minutes. Increase the heat and stir in the spinach, a handful at a time, until wilted. Turn off the heat and let the soup stand for 10 minutes before serving. Ladle into big bowls and garnish with limes, radishes, and avocados, as desired.

vietnamese *pho* rice noodle soup
with beef

Rice sticks, or *banh pho,* are translucent, linguine-shaped dried noodles sold in Asian markets. This recipe for beef *pho* comes from Charles Phan, chef/owner of The Slanted Door in San Francisco. Phan's wife, mother, sister, brothers, aunts, uncles, and brothers-in-law (in all, 24 family members known as the "Phan Clan") work with him at the restaurant. Since Vietnamese food is so simply prepared, use the freshest, highest-quality ingredients you can for the best flavor.

5 pounds beef marrow or **knuckle bones**

2 pounds beef chuck, cut into 2 pieces

2 yellow onions, peeled and charred (see **NOTE,** page 109)

Two 3-inch pieces ginger, cut in half lengthwise and lightly bruised with the flat side of a knife, lightly charred (see **NOTE,** page 109)

¼ cup fish sauce

3 ounces rock sugar or **3 tablespoons granulated sugar**

10 whole star anise, lightly toasted in a dry pan

6 whole cloves, lightly toasted in a dry pan

1 tablespoon sea salt

1 pound dried ¹⁄₁₆-inch-wide rice stick noodles

5 to 6 ounces beef sirloin, slightly frozen, then sliced paper-thin across the grain

GARNISHES

½ yellow onion, sliced paper-thin

3 scallions, cut into thin rings

⅓ cup chopped fresh cilantro

1 pound bean sprouts

10 sprigs fresh Asian basil

1 dozen fresh saw-leaf herb leaves (optional)

6 Thai bird chiles or **1 serrano chile,** cut into thin rings

1 lime, cut into 6 thin wedges

Freshly ground black pepper

(continued)

In a large stockpot, bring 6 quarts water to a boil. Place the bones and beef chuck in a second pot and add water to cover. Bring to a boil and boil vigorously for 5 minutes. Using tongs, carefully transfer the bones and beef to the first pot of boiling water. Discard the water in which the meat cooked. (This cleans the bones and meat and reduces the impurities that can cloud the broth.) When the water returns to a boil, reduce the heat to a simmer. Skim the surface often to remove any foam and fat. Add the charred onions and ginger, fish sauce, and sugar. Simmer until the beef chuck is tender, about 40 minutes. Remove one piece and submerge it in cool water for 10 minutes to prevent the meat from darkening and drying out. Drain, then cut it into thin slices and set aside. Let the other piece of beef chuck continue to cook in the simmering broth.

When the broth has been simmering for about 1½ hours total, wrap the star anise and cloves in a spice bag (or piece of cheesecloth) and add to the broth. Let them infuse until the broth is fragrant, about 30 minutes. Remove and discard both the spice bag and onions. Add the salt and continue to simmer, skimming as necessary, until you're ready to assemble the dish. The broth needs to cook for at least 2 hours. (The broth will taste salty but will be balanced once the noodles and accompaniments are added.) Leave the remaining chuck and bones to simmer in the pot while you assemble the bowls.

To prepare the noodles, first soak them in cold water for 30 minutes and drain. Then bring a large pot of water to a rolling boil. When you're ready to serve (not before), place the noodles, 1 portion (2⅔ ounces) at a time, into a sieve and lower it into the boiling water. Using chopsticks or a long spoon, stir so the noodles untangle and cook evenly. Blanch just until they're soft but still chewy, 10 to 20 seconds. Drain completely, then transfer them to a preheated bowl. Cook the remaining noodles the same way, as needed for each portion. If you're cooking for several people, you may cook the noodles all at once by adding them directly to the pot of boiling water. Just make sure to serve them immediately.

To serve, place each portion of cooked noodles in preheated bowls. (If the noodles are not hot, reheat them in a microwave or dip them briefly in boiling water to prevent them from cooling down the soup.) Place a few slices of the beef chuck and the raw sirloin on the noodles. Bring the broth to a rolling boil; ladle about 2 to 3 cups into each bowl. The broth will cook the raw beef instantly. Garnish with the yellow onion, scallions, and cilantro. Serve immediately, inviting guests to garnish their bowls with the bean sprouts, herbs, chiles, lime juice, and pepper.

NOTE / To char ginger and onions, hold each piece of ginger with tongs directly over an open flame or place it directly on a medium-hot electric burner. While turning, char until the edges are slightly blackened and the ginger is fragrant, 3 to 4 minutes. Char the onions in the same way. Peel and discard the blackened skins of the ginger and onions, then rinse and add to the broth.

"cheap and tasty" pork and orange stew

SERVES
6

After so many years of cooking à la carte meals in restaurants, television host and author Michael Chiarello craved long-cooked, all-in-one dishes like this stew from his book, *At Home with Michael Chiarello*. He loves stews for their intense and rich flavors, because they can be prepared far in advance of his guests' arrival, and because they are nice and easy on the entertaining budget. Simmer the stew slowly to coax the tenderness out of this pork cut, which is not naturally tender. This stew is wonderful served atop risotto or soft cooked polenta, accompanied by a good Merlot.

1½ **pounds boneless pork shoulder,** cut into bite-sized chunks

Finely ground sea salt, preferably gray salt

6 **tablespoons extra-virgin olive oil,** or more if needed

1 **cup dry red wine**

1 **cup freshly squeezed orange juice**

2 **tablespoons Cointreau**

2 **teaspoons toasted fennel seeds**

6 **cups Chicken Stock** (page 13) or **broth**

1 **bay leaf**

1½ **tablespoons unsalted butter**

12 **ounces yellow-fleshed potatoes,** such as Yukon Gold, peeled and cut into ½-inch cubes

12 **pearl onions,** peeled

2 **cups stemmed fresh shiitake mushrooms,** quartered

12 **baby carrots**

1 **tablespoon minced garlic**

1 **tablespoon finely chopped fresh rosemary**

Freshly ground black pepper

2 **tablespoons finely chopped fresh flat-leaf parsley**

1 **tablespoon grated orange zest**

Season the pork well with 2 teaspoons salt. In a large sauce pan, heat 4 tablespoons of the oil over medium-high heat until it begins to smoke. (The generous amount of oil allows the meat to brown well. The excess will be drained off.) Working in batches if necessary to avoid crowding the pan, add the pork and let it brown on the first side before turning, then sauté until well browned all over, about 10 minutes total. Pour the contents of the pan into a sieve to drain the excess fat.

Return the pan to high heat and return the meat to the pan. Add the wine, orange juice, Cointreau, and fennel seeds. Stir and scrape the bottom and sides of the pan to loosen all the browned bits. Bring the mixture to a boil, then reduce the heat slightly and simmer until reduced by half, about 5 minutes. Add the stock and bay leaf, reduce the heat to low, cover, and simmer slowly until the meat is very tender, about 45 minutes.

About 15 minutes before the meat should be ready, heat the remaining 2 tablespoons oil with the butter in a large sauté pan over medium-high heat. Add the potatoes, onions, mushrooms, and carrots and sauté until all the vegetables are well browned, about 15 minutes. Adjust the heat so the vegetables brown but do not burn, adding more oil if necessary. Add the garlic and rosemary and sauté briefly, just to brown the garlic. Season to taste with salt and pepper.

Scrape the contents of the sauté pan into the stew. Cook the stew until the vegetables are tender and the flavors have blended, about 15 minutes more. Just before serving, stir the parsley and orange zest into the stew. Taste and adjust the seasonings, then serve.

pork and hominy stew

posole

SERVES **6** TO **8**

Chef Peter Hoffman is a dedicated advocate for small farmers and environmentally beneficial farming. At Savoy, his rustic, romantic New York City restaurant in a two-story building in SoHo, the menu features ingredients from sustainable farms. Some of these ingredients turn up in his posole, a pork and hominy stew that is a holiday tradition in Mexico and New Mexico. Every family has its own version, using a favored chile, a preferred quantity of tomatillos and onions, and a favorite cut of meat. This version, published in *The Niman Ranch Cookbook,* has a slightly nutty taste from the addition of pumpkin seeds. At the restaurant, he begins with dried whole corn kernels, but canned hominy is easier to find, simpler to use, and an acceptable substitute. If you can find canned hominy that is labeled *nixtamal maize,* use it as the corn flavor is much better. This stew takes about 4 hours to make start to finish.

8 ounces boneless pork shoulder

1 pound meaty pork bones or **fresh ham hock**

1 cup hulled pumpkin seeds

1 pound tomatillos, husked and rinsed

6 serrano chiles, stemmed

1 yellow onion, chopped

2 tablespoons bacon drippings or **olive oil**

2 cans (29 ounces each) **hominy,** drained

3 garlic cloves, chopped

1 tablespoon dried Mexican oregano

Kosher salt

Freshly ground black pepper

CONDIMENTS

1 small red onion, diced

1 avocado, peeled, pitted, and diced

2 limes, quartered

8 radishes, thinly sliced

¼ head green cabbage, shredded

Put the pork shoulder and bones in a stockpot and add 4 quarts water. Bring to a boil over high heat. Reduce the heat to medium-low and simmer uncovered, skimming away any foam that rises to the top, until the meat is tender, about 3 hours. Remove from the heat and let the meat cool in the broth for about 30 minutes.

Preheat the oven to 350 degrees F.

Spread the pumpkin seeds on a baking sheet. Put them in the oven and toast until aromatic, 5 to 7 minutes. Let cool.

Using tongs, transfer the meat to a plate. Skim away and discard any fat collected on the top of the broth.

Heat a large skillet over medium-high heat. Add the tomatillos and cook, turning and rolling with tongs, until the skins begin to blacken and blister, about 5 minutes. Transfer them to a blender. Add the chiles to the skillet and cook, turning as needed, until the skins begin to blacken and blister, 1 to 2 minutes. Transfer them to the blender. Set the skillet aside.

Add 1 cup of the broth from the stockpot to the blender and blend until the tomatillos and chiles are finely chopped. Add the pumpkin seeds and blend until they are finely chopped. Add the onion and blend until almost puréed.

Heat the bacon drippings in the skillet over medium-high heat. Carefully pour the tomatillo purée into the skillet, watching for splatters. Cook until the purée begins to turn brown and dry slightly, about 10 minutes. Add it to the meat broth. Stir in the hominy, garlic, oregano, and 1 tablespoon salt. Shred the meat and add it to the vegetables. Cook over low heat until the flavors have melded, about 30 minutes. Season to taste with salt and pepper.

Put the red onion, avocado, limes, radishes, and cabbage in separate small bowls. Serve the stew with the condiments.

fish and shellfish
soups and stews

basque seafood and shellfish soup

ttoro

SERVES **4** TO **6**

Long ago, the Basques made "fish" soup by adding a few vegetables to the cooking liquid left after poaching salt cod. From that humble beginning blossomed Saint-Jean-de-Luz's sumptuous seafood soup brimming with rockfish, langoustine, mussels, and sometimes monkfish. Known as *ttoro* to the Basques, it occupies the same place in Basque cuisine as bouillabaisse does in Provence. This recipe was created by Gerald Hirigoyen, chef/owner of Piperade and Bocadillos restaurants in San Francisco, to celebrate his Basque heritage.

FISH BROTH

1 onion, coarsely chopped

1 carrot, coarsely chopped

2 stalks celery, coarsely chopped

1 small leek, white and light green parts only, coarsely chopped

12 garlic cloves, crushed

⅓ cup olive oil

3 pounds fish heads and trimmings

2 cups dry white wine

3 tomatoes, cored and quartered

Bouquet garni using 8 sprigs thyme, 2 sprigs flat-leaf parsley, 2 bay leaves, ½ teaspoon peppercorns

1 dried New Mexico chile, seeded, and halved

1 tablespoon black peppercorns

CROUTONS

½ day-old baguette

1 garlic clove

4 ounces dried sheep's milk cheese such as manchego or Swiss cheese, grated

⅓ cup olive oil

1 pound fresh hake fillets,
cut in thick medallions

1 pound boneless monkfish fillets,
cut in thick medallions

Kosher salt

Freshly ground white pepper

1 cup all-purpose flour

1 pound mussels,
washed and debearded

1 pound Manila clams,
well scrubbed

4 to 6 langoustines
(preferably with heads attached)

TO MAKE THE BROTH, in a stockpot or casserole, combine the onion, carrot, celery, leek, garlic, and oil over medium heat. Sauté until the vegetables begin to brown, about 5 minutes. Add the fish heads and trimmings. Cover and cook for 10 minutes, skimming the top occasionally. Add the wine. Cook until it reduces by half, about 8 minutes. Add 8 cups water, the tomatoes, bouquet garni, chile, and peppercorns. Bring to a boil. Reduce the heat, and simmer until flavorful, 45 minutes to 1 hour. Strain and set aside.

TO MAKE THE CROUTONS, heat the oven to 450 degrees F. Cut the baguette into 24 slices, about ⅓ inch thick. Rub both sides of each piece of bread with the garlic clove and lay it on a baking sheet. Sprinkle the cheese evenly over the top of the bread slices. Bake until the croutons are golden brown, 5 to 6 minutes.

TO MAKE THE SOUP, increase the oven temperature to 500 degrees F. Warm the oil to sizzling in a large sauté pan. Keeping them separate, sprinkle the hake and monkfish medallions with salt and pepper, and dredge them in the flour. First add the monkfish to the sauté pan. Brown the fish on each side for 1 to 2 minutes. Remove and drain on paper towels. Repeat with the hake. Bring the fish broth to a boil. Add the monkfish, hake, mussels, clams, and langoustines to the broth. Cover and put in the oven until the clam and mussel shells begin to open, 5 to 7 minutes. Discard any that do not open. Season with salt and pepper to taste and serve in large soup bowls, garnished with several croutons.

fish and shellfish soups and stews

cioppino

Peggy Knickerbocker, author of *Simple Soirees* and *The Ferry Plaza Market Cookbook*, recommends using a balance of shellfish and whitefish for this Genovese-inspired stew, a favorite of San Francisco's early immigrants. You can use whichever fish is in your area. If you don't want to clean and section a live crab, you can ask your fishmonger to do it for you. Serve with a green salad, crusty country bread, and a crisp white wine.

¼ **cup extra-virgin olive oil,**
plus extra for drizzling

1 **white onion,** chopped

½ **cup thinly sliced leeks,** white part only

4 **garlic cloves,** crushed

6 **anchovy fillets** or
2 **tablespoons anchovy paste**

⅓ **cup chopped fresh flat-leaf parsley**

4 **sprigs fresh marjoram**

½ **teaspoon red pepper flakes**

1 **live Dungeness crab** (2 to 2½ pounds),
cleaned and sectioned, crab fat reserved

8 **ounces lingcod** or other white fish

1 **cup dry white wine**

1½ **cups tomato purée** or **peeled,**
fresh whole tomatoes

8 **ounces clams,** well scrubbed

4 **ounces mussels,** scrubbed and debearded

8 **ounces raw prawns** or **large shrimp,**
peeled and deveined

8 **ounces calamari,** cleaned and
cut into rings and tentacles

Kosher or **sea salt**

Freshly ground black pepper

(continued)

fish and shellfish soups and stews

Warm the oil in a heavy, nonreactive pot over medium-high heat. Add the onion, leeks, and garlic and sauté until the garlic is golden. Add the anchovies, parsley, marjoram, and pepper flakes and stir to mix. Add the crab and fish and cook until the fish begins to fall apart, 7 to 10 minutes. Add the wine and cook to reduce the liquid by one-third.

Mix together the reserved crab fat, 1 cup water, and the tomato purée in a small bowl. Add to the pot, raise the heat to high, and bring to a boil. Add the clams, mussels, and prawns and cook until the clam and mussel shells begin to open and the prawns turn pink, approximately 3 minutes. Discard any clams or mussels that do not open. Add the calamari and cook until opaque, approximately 1 minute. Season to taste with salt and pepper. Ladle into soup bowls and drizzle with olive oil. Serve immediately.

fish soup
with peas, favas, and spring garlic

SERVES
6

This recipe comes from Gerald Gass, author of *The Olive Harvest Cookbook* and executive chef at McEvoy Ranch in Petaluma, California. Gerald recommends using several kinds of firm-fleshed white fish for the best flavor. Spring garlic is the immature garlic plant, harvested when it is less than an inch in diameter and before a bulb has formed at the base. The plants resemble leeks and should be cooked in the same way. They add a relatively mild garlic flavor to dishes, and make a flavorful addition to soups, stews, and mixed sautéed vegetables. If spring has passed or you can't find spring garlic, substitute a second leek. Serve the soup with a loaf of crusty bread and a nice bottle of wine—the same wine you used in the soup.

2 pounds young fava beans

1 large leek, white and light green parts only, split lengthwise and sliced crosswise ⅛ inch thick

1 large yellow onion, diced

1 pound spring garlic, white and light green parts only, split lengthwise and sliced crosswise ⅛ inch thick

10 tablespoons extra-virgin olive oil, divided

1 teaspoon sea salt or **kosher salt**

1½ cups fruity, dry, white wine, such as a Sauvignon Blanc or an un-oaked Chardonnay, reduced to ¾ cup (see **NOTE**)

8 cups Fish Stock or **Fish Fumet** (found frozen in specialty gourmet shops)

1½ pounds assorted firm white fish fillets, such as halibut, monkfish, or cod, cut into 1-inch chunks

1 pound English peas, shucked

Shuck the favas from their pods. Peel the outer skin from one. If the skin comes off easily, peel the rest and set aside. Otherwise, blanch them in boiling water for 45 to 60 seconds, drain, put into a bowl of cold water, and then slip their skins off. Set aside.

In a large, heavy pot, combine the leek, onion, garlic, 4 tablespoons of the oil, and the salt over low heat. Cover and sauté the vegetables, stirring occasionally, until softened but not colored, 15 to 20 minutes.

Increase the heat to medium-high and add the reduced wine and stock. Bring to a boil. Add the fish and reduce the heat to low. Simmer for 3 minutes, add the peas and fava beans, and continue simmering until the fish is opaque throughout and the vegetables are tender, about 3 minutes longer. Taste and adjust the seasoning. Ladle the soup into warmed bowls. Drizzle a tablespoon of oil into each bowl and serve immediately.

NOTE: To reduce the white wine, simmer over medium heat until liquid is "reduced" to ¾ cup.

crab and asparagus soup

SERVES **4** TO **6**

Long ago, when the French introduced white asparagus to Vietnam, local cooks used traditional cooking techniques to weave this new ingredient into their cuisine. In this recipe by Martin Yan, television host of *Yan Can Cook*, it is used in a soup that combines fresh flavors and contrasting textures. If you can't find canned white asparagus, increase the amount of fresh asparagus to 1½ pounds and cook all of the spears as directed in the first step.

10 fresh asparagus spears

1 tablespoon vegetable oil

2 green onions, chopped

1 teaspoon minced fresh ginger

5 cups Chicken Stock (page 13) or **broth**

1 can (15 ounces) **white asparagus,** drained
and cut on the diagonal into ½-inch pieces

8 ounces cooked crabmeat, flaked

3 tablespoons soy sauce

⅛ teaspoon white pepper

1 tablespoon cornstarch dissolved
in 2 tablespoons water

1 egg, lightly beaten

2 tablespoons chopped fresh cilantro

Trim off the tough ends from the fresh asparagus. Cut the spears into ½-inch pieces, leaving the tips in 1½-inch lengths. Bring a saucepan filled with water to a boil over high heat, add the asparagus, and cook until tender, 2 to 3 minutes. Drain, rinse with cold water, and drain again. Set aside the tips to use for garnish.

Place the same pan over medium-high heat until hot. Add the oil, swirling to coat the bottom. Add the green onions and ginger and cook, stirring until fragrant, about 30 seconds. Add the stock, cooked fresh asparagus, white asparagus, crabmeat, soy sauce, and pepper and bring to a boil over high heat. Add the cornstarch solution and cook, stirring, until the soup boils and thickens slightly, about 1 minute. Remove it from the heat and slowly drizzle in the egg while stirring constantly with a spoon to form egg flowers.

Ladle the soup into bowls, garnish with the reserved asparagus tips and the cilantro, and serve.

cream of asparagus soup
with oysters

SERVES
4

The classic, delicate flavors of oysters and asparagus combine to make this elegant yet unpretentious soup, by Chef Hubert Keller from Fleur de Lys restaurant in San Francisco. The soup can be made ahead, but it's important to reserve the oysters until you are ready to serve. Once you pour the soup over the oysters, their flavor will immediately infuse the dish, creating a deliciously sharp-edged combination of tastes. Don't reheat leftover oysters in the soup or their texture and flavor will be compromised. To reheat, strain and heat the soup, then add the oysters and cook just until heated through.

1 tablespoon extra-virgin olive oil

2 small leeks, white parts only, cut in half lengthwise and thickly sliced (about 1 cup)

1 quart Vegetable Stock (page 15) or **water**

¼ cup peeled and finely diced white potato

Salt

1 pound asparagus, cut into 4 or 5-inch slices

12 freshly shucked oysters, with their liquor reserved

Freshly ground black pepper

1½ tablespoons cream or **half-and-half**

4 sprigs fresh chervil

Heat the oil in a heavy-bottomed saucepan. Add the leeks and sauté over medium heat, stirring occasionally, until soft but not brown, 5 to 8 minutes. Add the stock, potato, and a pinch of salt, and bring to a boil. Reduce the heat to a simmer and cook for 10 minutes. Add the asparagus slices and simmer until the asparagus is tender, another 8 to 10 minutes.

Meanwhile, coarsely chop the oysters and place them in a bowl with the reserved oyster liquor. Set aside.

Transfer the soup to a blender and purée it until very smooth. Season with salt and pepper and strain through a fine-mesh sieve into a clean saucepan. Return the soup to a boil, stir in the cream, and adjust the seasonings if necessary. Divide the chopped oysters and their juices among 4 warm soup bowls, and ladle the soup over the oysters. Garnish with the chervil and serve.

hog island oyster stew

Located on the pristine waters of Tomales Bay, California, the Hog Island Oyster Company raises the best oysters in the West. Chefs Jessica and Kevin Scott serve this classic recipe at Hog Island's Oyster Bar at the San Francisco Ferry Plaza. The oysters cook very quickly, so don't overheat. Serve immediately.

20 shucked oysters, with their liquor
    reserved (about 12 ounces)

1½ cups cream

4 tablespoons (2 ounces) **unsalted butter**

2 tablespoons chopped fresh chives

Freshly cracked black pepper

Combine the oysters and their liquor, the cream, and butter in a saucepan. Cook over medium-high heat, stirring gently, until the butter is just melted. Ladle into bowls and garnish with the chives and pepper.

sour shrimp soup

Thai *tom yam goong*

SERVES
6

The three ingredients essential to this classic Thai soup by Joyce Jue, travel and food consultant and author of *Asian Flavors* and *Savoring Southeast Asia*, are lemongrass, galanga (also known as Siamese ginger), and kaffir lime leaves. They may be found in better Southeast Asian grocery stores. In recent years, the kaffir lime leaf's popularity has grown immensely with Western cooks. It is now available in some American supermarkets in the fresh herbs section of the produce department. To make certain that she always has this flavor and scent available, Joyce now has a kaffir lime plant to keep her happy.

12 ounces large (21 to 30 per pound) **raw shrimp**

2 tablespoons vegetable oil

6 cups Chicken Stock (page 13)
  or **canned low-salt chicken broth**

4 stalks fresh lemongrass, cut into 2-inch
  lengths and lightly crushed

6 quarter-size slices fresh galanga
  or **3 pieces dried galanga**

8 green serrano chiles or **Thai bird chiles,** halved

8 fresh, frozen, or **dried kaffir lime leaves,**
  spines removed

½ cup canned whole straw mushrooms, drained

1 tablespoon roasted chili paste (*nam prik pao*)

3 tablespoons Thai fish sauce (*nam pla*)

2 tablespoons freshly squeezed lime juice,
  or more to taste

1 red serrano chile, cut into rounds

2 tablespoons coarsely chopped fresh cilantro

Peel and devein the shrimp; reserve the shells. Heat the oil in a large saucepan. Add the shrimp shells and sauté until they turn bright orange, about 1 minute. Add the stock, lemongrass, galanga, green chiles, and 4 of the lime leaves; bring to a boil. Reduce the heat and simmer for 15 minutes.

With a large strainer, scoop out the shrimp shells and seasoning ingredients and discard. Add the mushrooms, chili paste, and fish sauce to the stock; bring it to a boil. Add the shrimp and remaining 4 lime leaves; cook until the shrimp turn bright orange, about 1 minute. Stir in the lime juice. Adjust the chili paste and fish sauce to taste. Ladle the soup into soup bowls. Garnish with the red chile and cilantro.

green-lipped mussels in coconut broth
with cilantro pesto

SERVES
6

Mussels and coconut milk together make one of Chef Cindy Pawlcyn's favorite flavor combinations. In this soup, the richness of the coconut milk carries the spicy flavors well. Cindy, the founding chef at Mustards Grill and Cindy's Back Street Kitchen in Napa, California, often serves it with a dry Gewürztraminer. It's especially great done in a pan over a fire at the beach, as the smoky aromas add to the overall yummy flavor. You may find that this cooks faster in two large sauté pans instead of a single soup pot.

CURRY BROTH

2 tablespoons extra-virgin olive oil

1 large (8 ounces) **yellow onion,** thinly sliced

2 to 2½ tablespoons minced garlic

2 tablespoons peeled, grated ginger

1 tablespoon Madras curry powder
dissolved in 1 tablespoon cold water

1 cup white wine

1 tablespoon honey

1½ quarts Chicken Stock (page 13) or **broth**

1 cup coconut milk

1 lime, juiced

CILANTRO PESTO

2 bunches fresh cilantro, stemmed

⅔ cup extra-virgin olive oil

2 tablespoons minced garlic

2 tablespoons chopped toasted almonds

1 tablespoon peeled, grated ginger

1 tablespoon minced jalapeño chile

1 tablespoon honey

¼ to ½ teaspoon white pepper

1 to 1½ teaspoons salt

Freshly squeezed lime juice, to taste

2 tablespoons extra-virgin olive oil

2 large (1 pound) **red onions,** thinly sliced

2 large (1 pound) **red bell peppers,** julienned

½ bunch scallions, julienned

8 ounces carrots, peeled and julienned

4 pounds green-lipped or black mussels,
scrubbed and debearded

(continued)

fish and shellfish soups and stews

TO MAKE THE BROTH, heat the 2 tablespoons of oil in a skillet and add the yellow onion. Cover and sweat the onion until soft. Add the garlic and ginger, cook 1 minute. Add the curry powder mixture; cook 1 minute. Add the wine and honey. Simmer to reduce by two-thirds, about 5 minutes. Add the stock and bring the mixture to a boil. Skim off any fat. Reduce it by one-third, about 5 minutes. Add the coconut milk and bring it back to a boil. Add a little fresh lime juice and check the seasonings.

TO MAKE THE PESTO, combine the cilantro, oil, garlic, almonds, ginger, jalapeño, honey, salt, and pepper in a blender or food processor. Blend until smooth. Add the lime juice and taste; adjust the seasoning as needed. Refrigerate the pesto, covered with plastic, until ready to use.

To finish the dish, heat the second 2 tablespoons of oil in a large pot or Dutch oven over high heat. Add the red onions, bell peppers, scallions, and carrots and cook until softened but not discolored. Add the curry broth and mussels. Bring to a boil, then reduce the heat to maintain a simmer and cook, covered, until the mussels open, 8 to 10 minutes. Discard any mussels that do not open. Serve immediately in bowls, garnished with cilantro pesto.

clam soup with roasted garlic

SERVES
4

If you have roasted garlic, you can make this delicious, delicate soup from *How to Cook Everything*, by *New York Times* columnist Mark Bittman, in about twenty minutes. And it's easy because you don't have to shuck the clams; they are cooked in their shells in this soup.

1 head garlic, separated into cloves but not peeled

2 tablespoons olive oil, divided

1 large onion, minced

4 cups Fish Stock (page 14), **Chicken Stock** (page 13), or **broth,** preferable warmed

24 littleneck or **other hard-shelled clams,** well scrubbed

1 orange, zested

2 limes, juiced, plus **1 lime,** cut into small wedges

Salt

Freshly ground black pepper

Minced fresh cilantro leaves, for garnish

1 small fresh chile, such as jalapeño, stemmed, seeded, and minced (optional)

Preheat the oven to 350 degrees F. Place the garlic cloves in a small, oven-proof bowl with 1 tablespoon of the oil. Cover with aluminum foil and roast until tender, about 1 hour. Cool.

Squeeze the garlic meat from its husks and reserve. Place the remaining 1 tablespoon of oil in a large, deep saucepan and turn the heat to medium-high. A minute later, add the onion and cook, stirring, until soft, about 5 minutes.

Add the stock and bring to a boil. Turn the heat to low. Add the clams, cover, and cook until they open, 5 to 10 minutes. Discard any clams that do not open.

Add the roasted garlic, orange zest, lime juice, salt, and pepper to taste. Stir and taste for seasoning. Garnish with cilantro and serve immediately, passing the lime wedges and the chile at the table.

clam chowder

On Cape Cod, there are as many recipes for clam chowder as there are clams in the sea. This recipe by Lora Brody, author of *The Cape Cod Table*, takes the very best elements of several dozen versions and puts them together to make a creamy, rich meal in a bowl that even New Yorkers will have to admit beats anything with tomatoes.

While you can certainly start by digging and shucking your own clams, most fish stores and many supermarkets sell shelled, chopped clams—Lora's preference. While some recipes call for using flour to thicken clam chowder, Lora doesn't like to use any thickener at all, so those of you used to the thick consistency of many commercial varieties will find this on the thinner side.

3 ounces salt pork or **thick slab bacon,** diced

1 large yellow onion, chopped in medium dice

3 stalks celery (with leaves), cut in small dice

3 cups peeled and diced Idaho potatoes

4 cups bottled clam juice

1½ pints (3 cups) **fresh chopped clams,** drained, liquor reserved

4 cups light cream

2 cups whole milk

Salt

Lots of freshly ground black pepper

8 tablespoons (4 ounces) **butter**

Paprika, for garnish

Cook the salt pork in a heavy skillet over medium heat, stirring occasionally. When the meat is brown and crisp, use a slotted spoon to remove it to a paper towel to drain.

Add the onion and celery to the drippings and cook over medium heat, stirring frequently, until they are wilted and the onion golden. Use the slotted spoon to add the cooked meat and vegetables to a soup pot. Discard the fat in the sauté pan and scrape any of the brown drippings that remain into the pot. Add the potatoes and clam juice (both bottled and that reserved from the fresh clams). Set the pot over high heat, cover, bring to a rapid simmer, then reduce the heat and cook until the potatoes are tender, 15 to 20 minutes. Stir in the cream and milk and heat, uncovered, without allowing the mixture to boil. When the mixture is hot, add the clams and cook for another 5 minutes (without boiling). Season to taste with salt and pepper. Serve immediately by ladling the chowder into heated bowls, garnished with a pat of butter and a sprinkling of paprika.

fish and shellfish soups and stews

salmon and corn chowder
with fresh herbs

When salmon is in season and fresh corn is piled high at the farmers' market, Diane Morgan, author of *Salmon: The Cookbook*, is inspired to make a chunky soup. The weather might be warm, but all it takes is a cool evening breeze to put her in the mood for a one-pot meal served with a crusty baguette and simple salad. In this recipe, she skillet-toasts the fresh corn for added depth of flavor. If you are into trimming calories, you can use as little as one strip of bacon and still get that bacon taste, and milk can be substituted for the half-and-half (just don't let the chowder come to a boil).

2 ears fresh corn

½ teaspoon kosher or **sea salt**

3 strips bacon, finely chopped

1 yellow onion, chopped

2 russet potatoes, peeled and cut into ½ -inch cubes

2 cups bottled clam juice or **Fish Stock** (page 14)

2 cups half-and-half or **milk**

1 salmon fillet (about 8 ounces), skin and pin bones removed, halved lengthwise and cut crosswise into thin slices

1 tablespoon minced fresh thyme

⅓ cup minced fresh flat-leaf parsley

Freshly ground black pepper

Husk the corn and remove all the silk. Trim the bottom end of the cobs so they are even. To remove the corn kernels from the cobs, stand an ear of corn upright in a wide, flat-bottomed bowl or on a work surface, and with a sharp knife, cut downward along the corn. Reserve the kernels and discard the cobs.

Heat a dry nonstick skillet over medium heat. Add the corn and sauté until the kernels are lightly browned and toasted, about 3 minutes. Stir in the salt, then remove the pan from the heat and set aside.

Cook the bacon in a heavy soup pot over medium heat until crisp, about 5 minutes. Using a slotted spoon, transfer the bacon to paper towels to drain. Pour off all but 2 tablespoons of the fat from the pan. Add the onion and sauté over medium heat for 1 minute, then cover and cook until soft but not brown, about 3 minutes. Add the potatoes and clam juice. Bring to a boil. Reduce the heat to low, cover, and simmer until the potatoes are tender, 10 to 12 minutes.

Add the corn, bacon, half-and-half, salmon, and thyme to the pot. Cook just below a simmer until the salmon is cooked through, about 5 minutes. (The half-and-half will curdle if the soup comes to a boil.) Add the parsley and season to taste with pepper. Serve immediately.

fish and *shellfish soups* and *stews*

shrimp, corn, and potato chowder

SERVES **6** AS AN APPETIZER; **4** AS A MAIN COURSE

This delicious chowder by Barbara Scott-Goodman, author of *The Beach House Cookbook*, is excellent to serve as a starter or as a main course for dinner. The shells of the shrimp are used in making the rich chowder broth, so ask your fishmonger to reserve them for you when cleaning the shrimp.

1 tablespoon olive oil

1 tablespoon unsalted butter

2 medium leeks, well rinsed and drained, white and green parts finely diced

4 cups Chicken Stock (page 13) or broth

1½ pounds red new potatoes (about 6 small), cut into ¼-inch dice

1 pound medium (31 to 35 a pound) raw shrimp, peeled and deveined, shells reserved

½ cup whole milk

1 cup half-and half

2 cups cooked corn kernels (from 3 ears fresh corn)

Kosher salt

Freshly ground black pepper

Minced fresh chives, for garnish

Heat the oil and butter in a skillet over medium heat. Add the leeks and cook until softened, about 5 minutes. Transfer the leeks to a large soup pot. Add the stock, 2 cups water, and the potatoes. Stir gently to combine.

Wrap the reserved shrimp shells in cheesecloth tied closed with kitchen twine. Bring the soup to a boil and drop the cheesecloth pouch into the pot. Reduce the heat, cover, and simmer until the potatoes are just tender, about 15 minutes.

Remove the cheesecloth pouch and discard. Add the milk and half-and-half, cover, and cook until heated through, about 5 minutes. Add the shrimp, corn, and salt and pepper to taste. Cook, uncovered, until the shrimp turn pink, stirring occasionally, 5 to 7 minutes. Taste and adjust the seasonings, if necessary.

Ladle the soup into shallow bowls and garnish with the chives. Serve at once.

poblano, tomatillo, and shrimp chowder
with hominy

SERVES 6 TO 8

This hearty, unusual soup by John Ash, author of *From the Earth to the Table* and *John Ash: Cooking One on One*, could be the centerpiece of a meal. The smoky flavor of the poblano chile is even better if you char-roast it before adding it. If poblanos are not available, Anaheim chiles can be substituted. Canned hominy is fine but if you can cook your own from dry corn, the flavor is much better. A good source for dry hominy or posole in several colors is Purcell Mountain Farms (www.purcellmountainfarms .com), who have a wonderful assortment of hominys and heirloom beans. The spicy, citric flavors of the tomatillos and the mild heat from the poblanos are delicious matched to a fruity Johannesberg Riesling or Gewürztraminer that is fresh and fruity with a bit of residual sugar.

2 tablespoons olive oil

1 pound yellow onions, halved and sliced lengthwise

4 medium, fresh poblano chiles, stemmed, seeded, and sliced into thin strips

1 tablespoon finely slivered garlic

7 cups Chicken Stock (page 13), Vegetable Stock (page 15), or broth

3 cups husked and halved fresh tomatillos

1½ cups diced, seeded tomatoes (drained if using canned)

2 teaspoons dried oregano (preferably Mexican)

½ teaspoon fennel seeds

½ teaspoon cumin seeds

½ teaspoon coriander seeds

¼ teaspoon ground cinnamon

Kosher salt

Freshly ground black pepper

Freshly squeezed lime juice

12 ounces medium (31 to 35 per pound) raw shrimp, peeled and deveined

¾ cup cooked, drained white hominy (posole)

¼ cup chopped fresh cilantro leaves, plus fresh cilantro sprigs, for garnish

Thinly sliced avocado, for garnish

In a large saucepan, heat the oil over medium heat. Add the onions, poblanos, and garlic. Sauté until soft but not brown, about 5 minutes. Add the stock, tomatillos, tomatoes, oregano, fennel, cumin, coriander, and cinnamon. Simmer gently for 15 minutes. Season to taste with salt, pepper, and lime juice.

To serve, stir in the shrimp, hominy, and cilantro and simmer just long enough to cook the shrimp through, about 2 minutes. Ladle into warm soup bowls, garnish with the avocado slices and cilantro sprigs, and serve immediately.

dr. no's caribbean spicy seafood chowder

It's summer. It's the first weekend after the kids have left for camp. What better way to celebrate than by having a little Caribbean feast, the centerpiece of which is this spicy and succulent fish chowder by Bob Sloan, author of *Dad's Own Cookbook* and *The Tailgating Cookbook*. Like many dishes from the islands, this one has a lot of ingredients. But they all go in one pot, so it's not as challenging as it may at first seem. This became the favorite soup of one of James Bond's adversaries, Dr. No, after he settled down in Jamaica. He, of course, didn't need potholders, but some crusty Italian bread would be just grand.

12 littleneck clams

2 tablespoons cornmeal

4 slices thick-cut bacon, cut into ¹⁄₂-inch pieces

2 tablespoons olive oil

1 medium onion, finely chopped

2 carrots, diced

2 stalks celery, diced

4 scallions, finely chopped

6 garlic cloves, finely chopped

1 teaspoon chopped fresh ginger

1¹⁄₂ pounds snapper fillets or other firm-fleshed white fish, cut into 1-inch pieces

2 medium yams, peeled and cut into ¹⁄₂-inch pieces

4 cups Chicken Stock (page 13) or **broth**

1 can (14¹⁄₂ ounces) **crushed tomatoes**

1 cup bottled clam juice

¹⁄₄ cup dark rum

¹⁄₄ cup sherry or **port**

¼ cup chopped fresh parsley

3 tablespoons Pickapeppa or other hot sauce

½ teaspoon ground allspice

¼ teaspoon ground cloves

¼ teaspoon freshly ground nutmeg

1 bay leaf

12 ounces large (21 to 30 per pound) raw shrimp, peeled and deveined, tails left on

Salt

Freshly ground black pepper

Rinse the clams well under cold running water and transfer them to a bowl of cold water into which you've stirred the cornmeal. Let the clams sit until you need them.

Place a heavy-bottomed soup pot over medium-high heat. Add the bacon and cook until it is just beginning to crisp, about 2 minutes.

Pour out all but 1 tablespoon of the fat. Add the oil, onion, carrots, celery, and scallions and cook, stirring frequently, until the vegetables are soft, about 6 minutes. Add the garlic and ginger and cook 2 minutes more, stirring frequently.

Add the snapper, yams, stock, tomatoes, clam juice, rum, sherry, parsley, Pickapeppa, allspice, cloves, nutmeg, and bay leaf and bring the liquid to a boil. Reduce the heat, cover, and simmer for 20 minutes.

Drain the clams and add them to the pot along with the shrimp. Cook, covered, until the clams open up and the shrimp are cooked through, about 6 minutes. Discard any clams that do not open.

Season with salt and pepper to taste and serve.

acknowledgments

A good book is like a good soup, determined by the quality of its ingredients. We'd like to thank all the chefs and cookbook writers who so generously contributed to this book, and to Larry Bain for his vision for Nextcourse and for being such a great partner on this project. We'd also like to extend our heartfelt thanks to Bill LeBlond, director of cookbooks at Chronicle Books, whose great expertise, friendship, and continual support have been so essential to the larger expression of our work; to editor Amy Treadwell, whose input and passion guided this book to fruition; as well as to Amy Portello, whose recipe testing and research was invaluable, and to Ann Rolke, for her meticulous copyediting. We'd also like to thank designers Julia Flagg and Brett MacFadden for their lovely design. And finally, we'd like to thank our community of soup lovers everywhere who are brave enough to cast the first stone.

BRUCE AIDELLS

Bruce Aidells founded the Aidells Sausage Company in 1983, where he earned his reputation as "The Sausage King." He is the author of many cookbooks, including *The Complete Meat Cookbook*, *Bruce Aidells' Complete Book of Pork*, *Hot Links and Country Flavors*, and *Bruce Aidells' Complete Sausage Book*. Bruce has been featured in *Gourmet*, *Bon Appétit*, and *Food & Wine*, as well as on TV and radio cooking shows. He currently lives in the Bay Area with his wife, chef Nancy Oakes.

AYLA ALGAR

Ayla Algar is the author of *The Complete Book of Turkish Cooking* and *Classical Turkish Cooking*. She was born and raised in Turkey and is the Mellon Lecturer in Turkish at the University of California, Berkeley. Her recipes, articles, and tips have appeared in the *San Francisco Chronicle* food section.

JOEY ALTMAN

Joey Altman is best known for his two-time James Beard Foundation Award–winning food magazine–television show, *Bay Café*. He has also hosted *Appetite for Adventure* and *Tasting Napa* on the Food Network. Joey lives in San Francisco with his wife and three children and plays with other chefs in his band, Backburner's Blues Band. He is currently at work on a book. Learn more at www.joeyaltman.com.

JOHN ASH

John Ash is the author of several award-winning books, including *John Ash: Cooking One on One* and *From the Earth to the Table*. He also contributes to the Los Angeles Times Syndicate, *Bon Appétit*, and *Fine Cooking*. Ash's famed restaurant, John Ash & Company, is in Northern California. He currently serves on the faculty at CIA Greystone and is on the Board of Overseers for the Chef's Collaborative and the Board of Advisors of Seafood Watch. Find out more at www.chefjohnash.com.

JAN BIRNBAUM

Jan Birnbaum's training in Louisiana cooking with Paul Prudhomme and his upbringing in New Orleans inspired him to open his two restaurants, Catahoula in Calistoga and Sazerac in Seattle, both with Southern-inspired dishes. His expertise with Cajun and Creole dishes has influenced articles and stores that have been published in *Gourmet*, the *New York Times*, and the *Wall Street Journal*. Birnbaum's newest restaurant, Epic Roadhouse, is set to open in San Francisco in early 2007.

MARK BITTMAN

Mark Bittman writes the *New York Times* column "The Minimalist" and is the author of the award-winning, best-selling cookbook *How to Cook Everything* and the TV show *How to Cook Everything: Bittman Takes on America's Chefs* (which is also now a book). Bittman regularly appears on the *Today* show and NPR's *All Things Considered*, as well as countless other radio and television shows. More information on Mark and his show can be found at www.howtocookeverything.tv.

GEORGEANNE BRENNAN

Georgeanne Brennan is an award-winning author of many books, including *Potager, The Food and Flavors of Haute Provence, Great Greens*, and *A Pig in Provence*. She regularly contributes to *Bon Appétit, Metropolitan Home, Fine Cooking*, and *Eating Well*, and writes features for the *San Francisco Chronicle* food section. Her culinary vacation cooking school in Provence has been featured in *Gourmet, Food & Wine*, and *In Style*. She and her family split their time between Northern California and Provence. Learn more on Georgeanne at www.georgeannebrennan.com.

LORA BRODY

Lora Brody is the author of 23 cookbooks, including *Growing Up on the Chocolate Diet*, *The Cape Cod Table*, and *The New England Table*. She now makes her living as a Boston-based photographer. Occasionally, she teaches cooking at La Combe in Perigord in France and makes special appearances at her son Max Brody's restaurant, The Night Kitchen, in Montague, Massachusetts. Brody's photographs can be found at **www.lorabrody.com**.

LINDA CARUCCI

Linda Carucci is the author of *Cooking School Secrets for Real World Cooks*, inspired by classes she taught around the country. She was recently awarded the honor of Cooking Teacher of the Year by the International Association of Culinary Professionals. In addition to teaching, she is the Julia Child Curator and Food Consultant of Food Arts at COPIA: The American Center for Wine, Food, and the Arts in Napa. To learn more, visit **www.lckitchen.com**.

MICHAEL CHIARELLO

Michael Chiarello is the creative force behind and the television host of *NapaStyle* and *Easy Entertaining with Michael Chiarello*. He is the author of *At Home with Michael Chiarello*, *Michael Chiarello's Casual Cooking*, and *The Tra Vigne Cookbook*. He and his family live in Napa Valley. More information about Michael and NapaStyle can be found at **www.napastyle.com/Michael**.

CAT CORA

Cat Cora was featured as an Iron Chef on Food Network's *Iron Chef America*. She is the author of *Cat Cora's Kitchen* and the weekly column "Cooking from the Hip," which will soon be published as a book, for the *Contra Costa Times*. She co-founded Chefs for Humanity, a grassroots coalition of chefs dedicated to raising funds for humanitarian aid and hunger-related initiatives throughout the world.

MARY CORPENING BARBER AND SARA CORPENING WHITEFORD

Thymes Two partner, Mary Corpening Barber and Sara Corpening Whiteford have been cooking together since the age of five. They have each worked in some of the country's most celebrated restaurants and have taught numerous classes at cooking schools and gourmet food shops nationwide. Together, they have sold over a million books, including *Smoothies*, *Simplify Entertaining*, *Cocktail Food*, and *The Bride & Groom First and Forever Cookbook*.

DANA COWIN

Dana Cowin has been *Food & Wine*'s editor in chief since 1995, overseeing trends in food, drink, entertainment, travel, and design for millions of readers. Previously, she was an executive editor of *Food & Wine*, and an editor at *Mademoiselle*, *HG*, and *Vogue*. She is on the board of directors for City Harvest, a New York City hunger relief organization. She also serves as a member of the American Society of Magazine Editors, The International Association of Culinary Professionals, and The American Institute of Wine & Food. Dana lives in Manhattan with her family.

MARION CUNNINGHAM

Marion Cunningham is the editor of the revised edition of *The Fannie Farmer Cookbook* and the author of *The Breakfast Book*, *The Supper Book*, *Lost Recipes*, and *Cooking with Children*, as well as numerous other titles. She is also the co-founder of the Baker's Dozen, was named scholar-in-residence by the IACP, and received the Grand Dame Award from Les Dames d'Escoffier. She has contributed articles to *Bon Appétit*, *Food & Wine*, and *Gourmet* magazines, as well as numerous other publications. She lives in Walnut Creek, California.

TRACI DES JARDINS

Traci Des Jardins is the co-owner and chef at Jardiniere, Acme Chophouse, and Mijita restaurants in San Francisco. After opening her own restaurant, she was named as a "best chef" by *Food & Wine* and the *San Francisco Chronicle*. She is dedicated to promoting local, sustainable agriculture and has been honored by the City of San Francisco for her efforts. Visit **www.tracidesjardins.com**.

SARA DESERAN

Sara Deseran is the senior food editor at San Francisco's *7x7* magazine. Previously, she was the food editor at both *Williams Sonoma Taste* and *San Francisco* magazine. Her writing has also appeared in the *San Francisco Chronicle*, the *New York Post*, *Gourmet*, *Food & Wine*, and *Every Day with Rachael Ray*. Sara is the author of *Asian Vegetables* and *Picnics* and co-author of *Sake*.

VANESSA DINA, KRISTINA FULLER, AND GEMMA DEPALMA

Vanessa Dina, Kristina Fuller, and Gemma DePalma are food lovers and amateur chefs who came together to develop *The Meat Club Cookbook: For Gals Who Love Their Meat!* to share their love of carnivore cuisine. Vanessa is a graphic designer who lives in San Francisco. Kristina is a recent mother living in Oakland, and Gemma works in the specialty food industry in New York City. People interested in learning more about these ladies and the Meat Club can visit **www.meatclubgirlsonly.com**.

ELIZABETH FALKNER

Elizabeth Falkner is the executive chef/owner at Citizen Cake in San Francisco, a unique bakery and restaurant known for contemporary cakes, chocolates, breads, pastries, and ice creams. She has been featured as one of the ten best pastry chefs in America in *Bon Appétit* and has also been profiled in *Pastry Art & Design*, *Gourmet*, *Food & Wine*, and *Travel & Leisure*. She has appeared on Food Network and Bravo's *Top Chef*. Her other restaurants, both in San Francisco, are Citizen Cupcake and Orson, a restaurant and bar set to open in 2007.

CAROL FIELD

Carol Field's award-winning books on Italian food include *In Nonna's Kitchen: Recipes and Traditions from Italy's Grandmothers*, *Focaccia*, *Italy in Small Bites*, *Celebrating Italy*, and *The Hill Towns of Italy*. Her love affair with the country began more than thirty years ago while working there with her husband. She is also the author of a novel titled *Mangoes and Quince*.

JANET FLETCHER

Janet Fletcher writes a regular food column for the *San Francisco Chronicle*. and has contributed to such publications as *Food & Wine*, *Bon Appétit*, *Fine Cooking*, and *Metropolitan Home*. She is also the coauthor of eighteen cookbooks, including *The Cheese Course*, *Fresh from the Farmers' Market*, *Four Seasons Pasta*, *Niman Ranch Cookbook*, and *Michael Chiarello's Casual Cooking*. Find out more at **www.foodwriter.com**.

GERALD GASS

Gerald Gass has worked as an executive chef at Square One in San Francisco, Catahoula in Calistoga, and most recently McEvoy Ranch in Marin County, California. At McEvoy, a 550-acre estate, his love for Mediterranean cuisine and appreciation for cultivation of foods has found full expression as he helps to develop olive groves of over 18,000 organically grown trees to make oil locally. Because of his experiences, Gerald has written *The Olive Harvest Cookbook*.

SUZANNE GOIN

Suzanne Goin is the co-owner, with partner Caroline Styne, of two acclaimed Los Angeles restaurants, Lucques and A.O.C. Her cookbook, *Sunday Suppers at Lucques,* won a James Beard Foundation Award, and she was awarded Best Chef, California, in 2006. She has also opened The Hungry Cat with her husband, chef David Lentz.

JOYCE GOLDSTEIN

Joyce Goldstein is a prolific cookbook author, cooking teacher, and lecturer. As the former chef/owner of Square One restaurant in San Francisco, Goldstein won many honors for her innovative Mediterranean cooking. Her award-winning cookbooks include *The Mediterranean Kitchen, Back to Square One, Kitchen Conversations, Solo Suppers, Cucina Ebraica: Flavors of the Italian Jewish Kitchen, Saffron Shores,* and *Italian Slow and Savory.*

GABRIELLE HAMILTON

Gabrielle Hamilton is the chef/owner of Prune in New York City, which has been named a world's-best restaurant by several publications. In addition, Hamilton works as a food writer, contributing to publications including the *New Yorker,* the *New York Times, Saveur,* and *Food & Wine.* Her work has been anthologized in *Best Food Writing 2001, 2002, 2003,* and *2004,* and her food memoir will be published in 2007.

JESSICA HARRIS

Jessica Harris is a cookbook author and culinary historian. She has traveled extensively, tracing the history of African food in the Americas, but always seems to come home to her native New York. She has a Ph.D. in performance studies and is a professor of English at Queens College, CUNY. She is the author of numerous books and cookbooks, including *The Africa Cookbook, Tasting Brazil,* and *Beyond Gumbo.* She also writes on food, travel, and culture for magazines including *Eating Well, Food & Wine, Essence,* and the *New Yorker.*

GERALD HIRIGOYEN

Gerald Hirigoyen is the executive chef and owner of Piperade, a California-Basque restaurant, and Bocadillos, a French-Spanish tapas bar, both in San Francisco. Both restaurants have received acclaim from food critics and magazines such as the *New York Times, Food & Wine,* and *San Francisco* for his simple, uncomplicated dishes. His cookbooks include *Bistro* and *The Basque Kitchen.* He lives in Mill Valley with his family.

PETER HOFFMAN

Peter Hoffman is the executive chef and owner of Savoy, the famous New York City restaurant. Both he and his restaurant are committed to using local, fresh ingredients and promoting sustainable food and farming. In addition to his work as a chef, he regularly contributes recipes to several publications, including *Food & Wine* and *The Green Guide.* His recipes have also appeared in *The Niman Ranch Cookbook.*

MADHUR JAFFREY

Madhur Jaffrey started her career as an actress before establishing her reputation as a leading authority on Indian cooking. Because she taught herself to cook, her simple, clear style of explanation has made her a hugely successful food writer and teacher. She has hosted several cooking shows on BBC television as well as writing books on Indian, Asian, and worldwide vegetarian cuisines. Her cookbooks include *Madhur Jaffrey's Indian Cookery, Madhur Jaffrey's Quick & Easy Indian Cooking,* and *Madhur Jaffrey's A Taste of the Far East.*

PHILIPPE JEANTY

Philippe Jeanty worked all over the world before settling in California's Bay Area. He began his career in the area by opening the Domaine Chandon winery's restaurant in Napa Valley and developed his own style of French bistro fare. Now, he is the owner of the acclaimed Bistro Jeanty, serving traditional French cuisine in Yountville, California. He is also chef/owner of Jeanty at Jack's in San Francisco and PJ Steak House, also in Yountville.

SUZANNE JONATH

Suzanne Jonath is Leslie Jonath's mother. She's famous for her spicy lamb soup with cinnamon, orzo, lemon, and dates.

JOYCE JUE

Joyce Jue has been teaching and writing about Chinese and southeast Asian cuisine for more than twenty years. Her cookbooks include the IACP award-winning *Savoring Southeast Asia*, *Asian Appetizers*, *Far East Cafe*, *Wok and Stir Fry Cooking*, and *Asian Flavors*. She wrote the "East-to-West" food column for the *San Francisco Chronicle* for ten years and has contributed to the *San Francisco Examiner*, *Food & Wine*, *Cooking Pleasures*, *Wok Talk*, *The Restaurant Lover's Companion*, *Vancouver's City Foods*, and *Prodigy*.

BARBARA KAFKA

Few have done more to define how Americans prepare food than Barbara Kafka, whose IACP and James Beard Award–winning books, *Roasting: A Simple Art* and *Microwave Gourmet*, made two utilized techniques central to everyday cooking. Barbara is a former food editor of *Vogue* and a frequent contributor to the *New York Times*. She lives in New York and Vermont.

HUBERT KELLER

Hubert Keller is the executive chef and co-owner of San Francisco's Fleur de Lys restaurant and also serves as the consulting chef at the Club XIX at the Lodge in Pebble Beach. He has received a James Beard Award for Best Chef and was named one of the "10 Best Chefs" by *Food & Wine* magazine. He opened Burger Bar at Mandalay Place and Fleur de Lys Restaurant and Lounge at Mandalay Bay in Las Vegas.

LORETTA KELLER

Loretta Keller is the chef/owner of COCO500, a San Francisco restaurant that has been praised for its innovative use of small plates with French bistro cuisine. Keller commits to providing the best for her customers, supporting local farmers' markets and using many local ingredients in her dishes.

PEGGY KNICKERBOCKER

Peggy Knickerbocker is a San Francisco–based freelance food and travel writer. She contributes regularly to *Saveur* and has also written for *Gourmet*, *Food & Wine*, *House & Garden*, the *San Francisco Chronicle*, and the *New York Times*. Her cookbooks include *Olive Oil From Tree to Table*, *The Rose Pistola Cookbook*, and *The Ferry Plaza Farmers' Market Cookbook*. She is also a cooking teacher and a board member of The Chez Panisse Foundation. To find out what she is doing now, visit her Web site at www.peggyknickerbocker.com.

JEFF KOEHLER
Jeff Koehler is the author of *La Paella: Deliciously Authentic Rice Dishes from Spain's Mediterranean Coast*. His food and travel writing has appeared in *Gourmet*, *Food & Wine*, *Eating Well*, the *Washington Post*, the *Los Angeles Times*, *Dwell*, and various other publications. He has also photographed two cookbooks, Teresa Barrenechea's *The Cuisines of Spain* and Braiden Rex-Johnson's *Pike Place Public Market Seafood Cookbook*. Jeff spends most of his time in Barcelona.

DEBORAH MADISON
Deborah Madison was the founding chef of Greens restaurant. She has written eight books, including *Vegetarian Cooking for Everyone*, *Vegetable Soups from Deborah Madison's Kitchen*, and *Local Flavors: Cooking and Eating from America's Farmers' Markets*. She serves on the Board of Seed Savers Exchange and is active in the Slow Foods movement. Deborah lives with her family in Galisteo, New Mexico. Learn more at www.deborahmadison.modwest.com.

TONY MANTUANO
Tony Mantuano is the James Beard Award–winning executive chef and partner of Spiaggia Italian and Café Spiaggia in Chicago. He also runs his own restaurant, Tuttaposto, and his family's restaurant, Mangia, in Wisconsin. Tony is the author, with Cathy Mantuano, of *The Spiaggia Cookbook: Eleganza Italiana in Cucina*. Beyond just cooking, he also teaches classes and gives demonstrations in Italian cuisine.

NANCIE MCDERMOTT
Nancie McDermott is a food writer and cooking teacher specializing in the cuisines of southeast Asia. Her stories and recipes have appeared in numerous national magazines, and her cookbooks include *Real Thai: The Best of Thailand's Regional Cooking*, *Real Vegetarian Thai*, and *Quick & Easy Vietnamese*. Nancie is frequently a guest teacher at cooking schools around the country. She lives in Chapel Hill, North Carolina.

DIANE MORGAN
Diane Morgan is an award-winning cookbook author and freelance food writer. She regularly contributes a column for the *Los Angeles Times* and writes for many food magazines such as *Bon Appétit* and *Fine Cooking*. She is the author of eleven cookbooks, including *Cooking for the Week*, *Dressed to Grill*, *The Thanksgiving Table*, and *Midnight Munchies*. She lives in Oregon. Check out her Web site at www.dianemorgancooks.com.

KITTY MORSE
Kitty Morse was born in Casablanca, Morocco. She has taught Moroccan cooking for more than twenty years and is the author of numerous cookbooks, including *The Scent of Orange Blossoms*, *Cooking at the Kasbah*, *Couscous*, *The California Farm Cookbook*, and *The Vegetarian Table: North Africa*. Kitty has appeared on public radio, the Food Network, CNN, and all major networks. Her recipes have been featured in *Cooking Light*, *Fine Cooking*, *Sunset*, *Bon Appétit*, and many others. She lives in Southern California. Find out more at www.kittymorse.com.

JOAN NATHAN

Joan Nathan has spent most of her career studying ethnic foods, specifically Jewish foods and the roots of the foods of the Middle East. She is the author of nine cookbooks, including *Jewish Cooking in America, The Jewish Holiday Kitchen,* and *The Foods of Israel Today.* Her newest book, *The New American Cooking,* looks at the many innovators and inventions that have shaped American food over the past forty years. She has also had a PBS TV series, *Jewish Cooking in America with Joan Nathan,* which was nominated for a James Beard Award.

MICHEL NISCHAN

Michel Nischan has pioneered his full-flavored, healthful cuisine as executive chef of Heartbeat restaurant in New York City. He is the author of the James Beard Award–winning *Taste Pure and Simple* and *Homegrown Pure and Simple.* He contributes to many magazines and TV shows, including *The Oprah Winfrey Show* and several on the Food Network. Michel is a founding member of the New American Farmer Initiative. He lives with his family in Connecticut. Find out more at www.michelnischan.com.

ROLAND PASSOT

Roland Passot is the chef/owner of La Folie and of the Left Bank restaurants in California's Bay Area. His distinctive dishes reflect a Franco-Californian sensibility, which he has brought to restaurants all over the country, including Le Francis in Chicago, The French Room at the Adolphus Hotel in Dallas, and Le Castel in San Francisco.

CINDY PAWLCYN

Cindy Pawlcyn is the chef/owner of Mustards Grill and Cindy's Back Street Kitchen in Napa Valley, California. She is the author of numerous cookbooks, including *Fog City Diner Cookbook,* the James Beard Award–winning *Mustards Grill Napa Valley Cookbook,* and *Big Small Plates.* To find out more about Cindy and her restaurants, visit her Web site at www.cindysbackstreetkitchen.com.

JACQUES PÉPIN

Jacques Pépin has hosted several TV cooking shows, including *Jacques Pépin: Fast Food My Way, Jacques Pépin Celebrates,* and *Julia and Jacques Cooking at Home (*with Julia Child), all of which have award-winning companion cookbooks. He has several other books, including *Simple and Healthy Cooking.* He participates in culinary festivals and fundraising events, and serves on the James Beard Foundation board. Learn more at www.jacquespepin.net.

SARA PERRY

Sara Perry is the author of numerous cookbooks, including *Everything Tastes Better with Garlic, Everything Tastes Better with Bacon, The New Complete Coffee Book, The New Tea Book,* and *Weekends with the Kids.* She lives in Portland, where she is a columnist and radio restaurant commentator for the *Oregonian.* To find out more about her work, visit www.saraperry.com.

CHARLES PHAN

Charles Phan is the owner and executive chef of The Slanted Door, a nationally recognized and extremely popular restaurant in San Francisco. There he and his family create upscale Vietnamese food with natural, local ingredients. He recently launched Out the Door, where loyal customers can take away their favorite dishes. In 2004, he earned the James Beard Award for Best Chef, California.

RUTH REICHL
Ruth Reichl is the editor in chief at *Gourmet* magazine. She has also worked as a restaurant critic at the *New York Times* and the food editor and restaurant critic for the *Los Angeles Times*. She has authored the acclaimed, best-selling memoirs *Tender at the Bone, Comfort Me with Apples,* and *Garlic and Sapphires*. Ruth lives in New York with her husband and son.

ALISON RICHMAN
Alison Richman has worked for several famed restaurants in California's Bay Area, including Jardiniere, with chef Traci Des Jardins, and XYZ (at the W Hotel) in San Francisco and Tantillo's in Burlingame. She currently works as a private chef to Steve Wynn.

TORI RITCHIE
Tori Ritchie is a San Francisco–based food writer and cooking teacher. She appears on "5-Minute Cooking School" on CBS's *The Early Show* and also hosted *Ultimate Kitchens* on the Food Network. She is the author of *Party Appetizers: Small Bites, Big Flavors* and *Braises and Stews: Everyday Slow-Cooked Recipes*. Ritchie serves on the advisory committee of Food Runners, a nonprofit organization that delivers food to the needy in San Francisco.

JUDY RODGERS
Judy Rodgers spent a year at a three-star restaurant in Roanne, France, where she learned the love of her craft. She is the James Beard Award–winning chef and co-owner of San Francisco's Zuni Cafe, also a James Beard Award winner. She is the author of the best-selling and James Beard Award–winning *Zuni Cafe Cookbook*.

RICK RODGERS
Rick Rodgers is a well-known cooking teacher, author, and TV personality. He has written more than twenty-five books, including the *101* series of cooking for beginners, *Fried and True, Pressure Cooking for Everyone, On Rice,* and *The Carefree Cook*. He has taught in America's best culinary schools, as well as in Korea and France. See more of Rick's projects at www.rickrodgers.com.

BETTY ROSBOTTOM
Betty Rosbottom is the author of *The Big Book of Backyard Cooking, Coffee,* and *Waffles*. She writes a syndicated column, "That's Entertaining," for Tribune Media Services and is a frequent contributor to Bon Appetit Magazine. When she's not writing or hosting a popular New England cooking show called On the Menu, she leads culinary tours to Europe. She lives in Amherst, Massachusetts.

JESSICA AND KEVIN SCOTT
Jessica and Kevin Scott are committed to serving fresh oysters from Tomales Bay, California, and promoting sustainable aquaculture. Their fresh, quality oysters and casual style of service at Hog Island's Oyster Bar at the San Francisco Ferry Building have made their restaurant one of the most prominent seafood restaurants in the city.

BARBARA SCOTT-GOODMAN

Barbara Scott-Goodman is a New York–based author, art director, and book designer with a specialty in cookbooks. She is the author and producer of *The Beach House Cookbook* and *Sensational Salads*, as well as the designer and producer of *The Garden Entertaining Cookbook; Picnics: Elegant Recipes for Alfresco Dining; Sunday Dinner; Autumn Nights, Winter Mornings;* and *Spring Evening, Summer Afternoon.* Her books and articles have been featured in such magazines as *Bon Appétit, Cook's Illustrated, House Beautiful, People,* and *Country Home.*

BOB SLOAN

Bob Sloan is the celebrated author of *Dad's Own Cookbook, The Working Stiff Cookbook, Great Burgers,* and *The Tailgating Cookbook.* He is also the co-author of *Hi-Fi's and Hi-Balls* and *A Stiff Drink and a Close Shave.* His humor pieces and fiction have appeared in *Playboy* magazine. Bob lives in New York City with his family, where he cooks, teaches, and writes mysteries. To see more of his work, visit www.bobsloansampler.com.

ANNIE SOMERVILLE

Annie Somerville is the author of *Fields of Greens* and *Everyday Greens.* She currently serves as the executive chef of Greens Restaurant in San Francisco, where she's committed to using garden fresh, local, organic produce and cooking with the seasons. Thanks to her guidance, Greens has flourished and expanded into a leading innovator of vegetarian cuisine. Annie works closely with the organic gardeners at Green Gulch Farm, as well as other local growers, when planning menus at Greens.

MARLENA SPIELER

Marlena Spieler is a broadcaster, journalist and food personality who writes the James Beard Award–winning *San Francisco Chronicle* column "The Roving Feast." She regularly contributes to magazines and newspapers worldwide, including *Saveur, Bon Appétit, Gambero Rosso,* and the *New York Times.* Her books include *Macaroni & Cheese* and *Grilled Cheese: Fifty Recipes to Make You Melt.* Marlena divides her time between San Francisco and the south of England. To learn more, visit www.marlenaspieler.com.

JESSICA STRAND

Jessica Strand is a Los Angeles–based food and lifestyle writer who has contributed to numerous publications, including the *Los Angeles Times, Bon Appétit, Vogue Australia, In Style, Self,* and *Wine & Spirits.* She is the author of *Dinner Parties, Intimate Gatherings, Salad Dressings,* and *Holiday Cocktails.* In addition to writing, Jessica is involved in developing food education programs for inner-city families.

JOANN TATUM

JoAnn Tatum is the mother of Frankie Frankeny. She is famous for her spicy chili.

CHARLIE TROTTER

Charlie Trotter is owner of Charlie Trotter's restaurant in Chicago, as well as Trotter's To Go, also in Chicago, and C in Los Cabos, Mexico. Trotter has had a TV cooking show on PBS, *The Kitchen Sessions with Charlie Trotter,* and has written numerous cookbooks and memoirs, including *Charlie Trotter Cooks at Home.* He was honored Humanitarian of the Year in 2004 for his work helping students through the Charlie Trotter Culinary Education Foundation.

ALICE WATERS

Alice Waters, owner of Chez Panisse in Berkeley, California, is the author of numerous best-selling cookbooks, including *The Chez Panisse Café Cookbook*. She has championed small, local, organic farms and ranches for more than three decades. She and her restaurant are credited for helping change the food landscape in the United States, as well as promoting the use of local, organic ingredients worldwide. She currently works promoting Edible Schoolyard programs by teaching students issues of nutrition and sustainability in Berkeley and trying to add these ideas to the city's academic curriculum.

JOANNE WEIR

Joanne Weir is the creator and host of several TV cooking shows, including *Weir Cooking in the Wine Country*, and *Weir Cooking in the City*, both of which have award-winning companion cookbooks. Her other cookbooks include *From Tapas to Meze, You Say Tomato*, and *Weir Cooking: Recipes from the Wine Country*. Joanne is also a cooking teacher and was awarded the IACP Julia Child Cooking Teacher Award of Excellence in 1997. To learn more, visit **www.joanneweir.com**.

LAURA WERLIN

Laura Werlin is the IACP Award–winning author of *The New American Cheese, The All American Cheese and Wine Book*, and *Great Grilled Cheese*. She has appeared on Joey Altman's *Bay Café, Sara's Secrets* with Sara Moulton, *Martha Stewart Living*, and numerous other television and radio shows. She writes for *Food & Wine, Fine Cooking, Cooking Light, Saveur, Cooking Pleasures*, and many other publications. She currently lives in San Francisco. Find out more at **www.laurawerlin.com**.

DIANE ROSSEN WORTHINGTON

Diane Rossen Worthington is a food writer, consultant, and James Beard Award–winning broadcaster who trained at the London Cordon Bleu Academy. She is the author of seventeen cookbooks, including *Seriously Simple, The Taste of the Season, The Taste of Summer, American Bistro*, and *The Cuisine of California*. She currently lives in Southern California. Learn more about Diane's work at **www.seriouslysimple.com**.

MARTIN YAN

Martin Yan is the host of more than 1,800 cooking show episodes, a certified Master Chef, a highly respected food consultant, a professional instructor, and a prolific, award-winning author. He is probably best known for his TV show, *Yan Can Cook*, where he brought authentic Asian cuisine into American homes. His books, including *Martin Yan Quick and Easy*, have also contributed to this. Even with his busy schedule, Yan manages and owns both casual and upscale pan-Asian restaurants worldwide.

table of equivalents

LIQUID / DRY MEASURES

U.S.	METRIC
¼ teaspoon	1.25 milliliters
½ teaspoon	2.5 milliliters
1 teaspoon	5 milliliters
1 tablespoon (3 teaspoons)	15 milliliters
1 fluid ounce (2 tablespoons)	30 milliliters
¼ cup	60 milliliters
⅓ cup	80 milliliters
½ cup	120 milliliters
1 cup	240 milliliters
1 pint (2 cups)	480 milliliters
1 quart (4 cups, 32 ounces)	960 milliliters
1 gallon (4 quarts)	3.84 liters
1 ounce (by weight)	28 grams
1 pound	454 grams
2.2 pounds	1 kilogram

OVEN TEMPERATURE

FAHRENHEIT	CELSIUS	GAS
250	120	½
275	140	1
300	150	2
325	160	3
350	180	4
375	190	5
400	200	6
425	220	7
450	230	8
475	240	9
500	260	10

LENGTH

U.S.	METRIC
⅛ inch	3 millimeters
¼ inch	6 millimeters
½ inch	12 millimeters
1 inch	2.5 centimeters
1 ounce (by weight)	28 grams
1 pound	454 grams
2.2 pounds	1 kilogram